HEADWAY

TEACHER'S BOOK   UPPER-INTERMEDIATE

John & Liz Soars

Oxford University Press

Note to teachers

Photocopies may be made, for classroom use, of pages 17–20 and 56–7 without the prior written permission of Oxford University Press. However please note that copyright law, which does not normally permit multiple copying of published material, applies to the rest of this book.

Oxford University Press
Walton Street, Oxford OX2 6DP

Oxford New York
Athens Auckland Bangkok Bombay
Calcutta Cape Town Dar es Salaam Delhi
Florence Hong Kong Istanbul Karachi
Kuala Lumpur Madras Madrid Melbourne
Mexico City Nairobi Paris Singapore
Taipei Tokyo Toronto

and associated companies in
Berlin Ibadan

Oxford and Oxford English are trade marks of
Oxford University Press

ISBN 0 19 433561 5

© Oxford University Press 1987

First published 1987
Eleventh impression 1996

Typeset by VAP Publishing Services, Kidlington, Oxford
Printed in Hong Kong

Description of the course

Headway Upper-Intermediate is the second volume of a comprehensive three-part course for students abroad and in the United Kingdom.

The aims of the course are to encourage students to analyse the systems of language in use, to expose them to a variety of challenging and interesting text-types in the listening and reading activities, and to bring their own experiences and feelings to the fore in order to achieve accurate and confident language use.

Headway is a revision and extension course which provides a compre-hensive coverage of the grammatical and lexical systems of English, combined with extensive practice of the four language skills in a communicative context. This volume can be used, with some supplementary examination-type exercises, to prepare students for the Cambridge First Certificate examination.

It provides approximately 120 hours' work, that is, ten hours per unit. The materials are organized in a way that makes *Headway Upper-Intermediate* suitable both for blocked courses, and for the traditional academic year.

Key-notes

Synthesis of accuracy and fluency

Often at this level, grammatical courses tend to be unstimulating, whilst those which provide interesting skills work do not present the grammar in a systematic, accessible manner. In *Headway*, detailed attention is given to both *language in*

parts (grammar and vocabulary) and *language as a whole* (in use for a real reason), thus achieving a cohesion of these two elements, providing a balance of aims for the teacher, and engaging the students both as language learners and as people with experiences and feelings of their own.

A test-teach-test approach to the grammar

At this level, students will have been introduced formally to many aspects of the language, and they will have encountered many more aspects informally in their reading and listening. Nevertheless, they continue to make mistakes of form and use, and few sentences that they speak or write are fully accurate. As at all levels, their receptive abilities exceed their productive ones.

In this volume of *Headway*, students are first exposed to the target language of a unit in the Discussion Point and the Reading activity (**test**). They are then directed to the Language Review and the Controlled Practice sections (**teach**). Finally, further skills work offers the opportunity for more practice and extension of the target language (**test**).

Comprehensive Grammar Reference section

As in *Headway Intermediate*, the Grammar section at the end of the book is like a condensed grammar book which can be used for reference purposes at any stage of the students' work. It can provide a preview of the language for preparation prior to a lesson, or a review for revision purposes. The grammar areas are dealt with in more depth than is usually

found in course books, but more concisely than is found in grammar books. The Grammar section is cross-referenced with each unit to provide more detailed information about the forms and uses of the language introduced.

Systematic lexical development

This course is unique in its approach to vocabulary development. Students at this level need to extend both their productive and their receptive vocabulary, and there are no easy routes to achieving this. The grammar of a language is a closed set, but the vocabulary is an open set, and therefore students must be encouraged to take as much responsibility for their own vocabulary learning as possible. There are at least two vocabulary exercises per unit in the Student's Book, and more in the Workbook. *Headway Upper-Intermediate* adopts a three-pronged approach to vocabulary development by:

- encouraging effective vocabulary learning strategies; for example keeping records, using reference works such as dictionaries and lexicons, and guessing the meaning of unknown words.

- introducing students to the systems of vocabulary, otherwise known as the 'grammar of vocabulary'; for example compound nouns, suffixes and prefixes, homonyms and homophones, synonyms and antonyms, multi-word verbs and collocation.

- introducing students to new words, both formally and informally: for example lexical sets such as those relating to illnesses and their symptoms and diagnosis; work;

ways of speaking, moving, and looking; and the language of statistics.

Skills development syllabus

As in *Headway Intermediate*, attention is paid to all four language skills, and the sub-skills of reading, listening, and writing are systematically introduced and practised.

Effective Teaching

For teachers, the key-note of *Headway* is its comprehensiveness and effectiveness. It has been designed to meet the practical lesson-to-lesson needs of the teacher. The units can be used chronologically to provide a balanced, cohesive timetable with the following components:

- opportunities for extensive skills work
- explanations of the target language
- controlled and freer practice of the target language
- extensive vocabulary work
- written homework assignments
- revision

This does not mean that teachers will not want to select and supplement, but when doing so they can rely on the book to combine thorough handling of input and skills development with variety of activity and control.

Effective Learning

For students, the key-note of *Headway* is accessibility and comprehensibility. It speaks directly to the students themselves. The contents page, headings, instructions, explanations, and cross-references are designed to guide students through the book with maximum understanding of what they have to do and why. If they are made aware of the aims of the course and the elements that constitute language acquisition, their contributions will be all the more relevant, and they can assume a considerable amount of responsibility for their own learning, both before, during and after the language lesson.

The organization of the course

Each unit of *Headway Upper-Intermediate* has ten sections, though not necessarily in the same order.

1 A Discussion Point, which launches the theme of the unit by means of a speaking activity. Often, this prompts use of the target language, so teachers can diagnose students' level of proficiency.

2 A Reading activity, which practises different reading skills, and which usually contains significant exponents of the target language.

3 Vocabulary 1, arising out of the theme of the unit, or the preceding material.

4 A Listening activity, which practises different listening skills, and which usually revises the target language, and/or contains significant exponents of further target language.

5 Vocabulary 2, arising out of the theme of the unit, or the preceding material.

6 A Speaking activity related to the theme, either a discussion or a roleplay.

7 A Writing activity, which focuses on one aspect of the writing skill.

8 The Language Review, which gives the essential rules of form and use of the target language.

9 Controlled Practice exercises which consist of pair and group work, comparing and contrasting sentences, writing, and sometimes listening.

10 A Revision section, which revises/introduces areas of the language that students at this level need to be familiar with.

The Language Review and the Controlled Practice exercises are cued after the Reading and the Listening activities, thus ensuring a balance in the timetable of fluency work (freer) and accuracy work (more controlled).

Naturally, teachers can choose the order in which they use the material. If they decide that their students are very unfamiliar with the target language of a unit, they might choose the following order:

- Language Review (accuracy)
- Controlled Practice (accuracy)
- Discussion Point (fluency)
- Reading (fluency)
- Vocabulary 1 (accuracy)

etc.

On the other hand, if teachers use the material as suggested, the stages are as follows:

- Discussion Point (fluency)
- Reading (fluency)
- Language Review (accuracy)
- Controlled Practice (accuracy)
- Vocabulary 1 (accuracy)

etc.

However, only individual teachers can know what best meets the needs of their particular students and the demands of the timetable.

The Language Review is cross-referenced to the Grammar section, which deals with the target language in greater depth. Further controlled practice exercises are contained in the Workbook.

Methodology

The *Headway* series encourages what is generally considered to be a communicative methodology. This is embodied in the following features:

- Students are challenged cognitively.
- They are involved in the learning process.
- They are asked to contribute their own opinions, experiences, and feelings.
- They take part in realistic activities.
- They are encouraged to work closely with peers.
- They are encouraged to assume a certain responsibility for their own learning, and to develop learning skills.

- The teacher adopts differing roles (informer, monitor, resource, consultant) according to the stage of the lesson.

Syllabus

There is no such consensus as to what constitutes a communicative syllabus. Any of the following syllabuses can be adapted to a communicative methodology:
- A structural syllabus, which introduces grammatical items under structural headings.
- A functional syllabus, which introduces grammatical items and phrases under functional headings.
- A task-based syllabus, which does not aim to introduce discrete language items consciously, but which consists of a sequence of activities or 'tasks'. Students acquire the target language in the process of performing these.

The *Headway* series incorporates all the above, but particularly the first in its accuracy-based work, and the last in its fluency-based work. In recent years, 'syllabus' has come to mean more than just the selection and grading of structural items. In *Headway*, many other elements in the language-learning process are selected and graded to form parallel syllabuses. These are:
- a grammatical syllabus
- a vocabulary-acquisition syllabus
- a reading syllabus
- a listening syllabus
- a speaking syllabus
- a writing syllabus
- a revision syllabus

Accuracy versus fluency

There has been much debate in recent years about the amount of attention that should be given to the *language in parts* as opposed to the *language as a whole*. The premise of the debate is that language proficiency is more than the sum of its parts, and that the isolation of a component part (for example, the Future Continuous, giving opinions, verbs to do with ways of cooking, rules of sentence stress, or the pronunciation of weak forms) and its controlled practice does not lead to mastery of the item when put back with the whole. No doubt enlightened teachers of all disciplines over many years have known that 'what they teach is not necessarily what their students learn'. Research has shown that students perhaps learn the forms of a language best when their attention is on the meaning, which suggests that the ideal conditions for second language learning are quite similar to those under which a first language is learnt. Because learning cannot be directly controlled, shaped, or influenced, and because it is a subconscious process, it is common nowadays to talk of language 'acquisition' rather than language 'learning'.

The accuracy versus fluency debate is probably impossible to resolve, because we can never know the ideal ratio for all levels and all students. Obviously at beginners' level there needs to be a lot of accuracy work (input of grammar, lexis, and functional exponents) because students have few resources for fluency work (freer practice, using the language in authentic contexts). Thereafter the problem can be seen in different ways. It could be argued that as students progress from intermediate to upper intermediate level, less time should be devoted to accuracy work and more and more to fluency work, thus exposing them to ever more 'real' language. **Somehow or other, it is argued, they acquire more language and become more accurate, so that at an advanced level little accuracy work is necessary at all.**

Alternatively, it could be argued that while there should indeed be a lot of fluency work at intermediate level for the reasons mentioned above, at upper intermediate and advanced levels the amount of accuracy work should not drop off, and might even be increased. If a successful balance between accuracy and fluency work has been achieved at intermediate level, students should be equipped with sufficient linguistic confidence and ability to 'survive' in a target-language environment and understand the gist of what is going on around them. Their language is probably still inaccurate, but they can make themselves understood, and they possess a certain vocabulary albeit not very wide or precise. At the beginning of the upper intermediate level, students should have a basic proficiency and an overview of the grammar, so maintaining or even increasing the amount of accuracy work might eliminate some of these mistakes and enrich their language repertoire.

In *Headway Upper-Intermediate*, there is slightly more accuracy work than in *Headway Intermediate*, with a greater emphasis on vocabulary and a Revision section. It is, of course, impossible to put an absolute percentage to the ratio, but at the higher level it is approximately 40 per cent accuracy and 60 per cent fluency.

Accuracy work

Grammatical syllabus

The grammatical syllabus of *Headway Intermediate* concentrates on verb forms, particularly tenses and modal verbs, and this is consolidated and extended in *Headway Upper-Intermediate*. As A. S. Hornby points out in the introduction to the *Oxford Advanced Learner's Dictionary of Current English*, 'For anyone who is learning to speak or write correct English, the most important word in a sentence is the verb'. It is hard to avoid basing so much input on verb forms because they go to make up an extremely complex area of the language. English tense usage is very subtle, and students make many mistakes of form and use.

Headway Upper-Intermediate revises all of the input of *Headway Intermediate* and extends students' understanding of the grammar, comparing and contrasting items as necessary. It begins with an overview of the tense system, then deals with one of the most difficult areas of the language for foreign students, the Perfect Aspect. Among the verb forms dealt with as the course progresses are indirect and tag questions, several future forms (English has more of these than most other languages), modal verbs expressing possibility, and **will** and **would** to express habit.

Apart from verb forms, the grammatical syllabus consists of gerunds and infinitives, quantifiers, relative clauses, participle clauses, intensifying adverbs, and articles. In general, the grammatical input becomes increasingly difficult as the course progresses.

Translation

In *Headway Intermediate*, the translation of significant items of the target language of each unit is formalized in the Language Review. This is as a further checking of learning. There is no such invitation to translate in *Headway Upper-Intermediate* Student's Book, as the authors do not consider it as essential at the higher level.

However, translation can still be an extremely valuable exercise for the following reasons:

- Students can think they understand what an item means but in fact be wrong. Translating it into their L1 shows this.
- Students' cognitive awareness of English compared to their own language is heightened.
- Many students no doubt translate either consciously or sub-consciously anyway, and formalizing this should ensure accuracy.

The Teacher's Book provides examples of sentences for translation if this is judged to be necessary and appropriate. They can be written on the board for students to translate in pairs or groups. This should not take too long – about five minutes should be enough.

Language Review – Grammar section

In each unit there is a Language Review which gives the essential rules of form and usage. At this stage the grammar is closely related to the context in which it was introduced, and students are referred either to the reading or the listening text in which the item occurred. There is a further reference to the Grammar section at the back of the book where the area is explored in more depth. The Grammar section also contains a detailed explanation of the role of aspect in English tense usage, and an overview of the Perfect and the Continuous aspects. The grammar is given such prominence for several reasons:

- It is the mechanism that generates the infinite number of sentences that we produce and receive.
- It is a tangible system, and can provide one element of a systematic approach to teaching a language.
- It develops students' cognitive awareness of the language. Language is rule-based, and conscious or sub-conscious knowledge of the rules is the key to 'generalizability' and creativity.
- It conforms to students' expectations of language learning, and meets an often-heard request for 'more grammar'.
- It will be of assistance to teachers in the planning of their lessons.

Vocabulary syllabus

The role of lexis in the curriculum has been re-evaluated in the past few years, and no longer is it the 'poor relation' to structure in the syllabus. In *Headway Upper-Intermediate* lexis is given a prominent place. There are at least two vocabulary exercises per unit in the Student's Book and two per unit in the Workbook.

There is a three-pronged approach to vocabulary development:

1 Encouraging effective vocabulary learning strategies. As there is so much vocabulary in a language, and as students' needs and interests vary, it is essential that the students' themselves assume the main responsibility for their vocabulary acquisition. The foundations for this are laid in the first two units of the Student's Book. In Unit 1, students are introduced to several ways of organizing their own vocabulary records. *How* they choose to do this does not matter, but the importance of evolving a method of some kind cannot be overstated. Without a conscious attempt to do something with the many words they encounter, it is unlikely that students' active and passive vocabulary store will increase significantly.

In Unit 2, students are given guidance in deducing the meaning of unknown words via linguistic and contextual clues.

Throughout the course, the use of dictionaries is encouraged, and several of the sub-skills of effective dictionary use are practised, for example: finding compound nouns; finding the correct definition in multiple entries; pronouncing words from the phonemic script and the stress marks; identifying the key word in idiomatic expressions to find the correct entry; guessing the meaning of a word from the example contained in the entry when the definition is not understood; and deducing the spelling of a word that has been heard but not seen.

2 Introducing students to the systems of vocabulary, otherwise known as 'the grammar of vocabulary'. This is important because it shows that the words of a language are not isolated and unrelated, but can form patterns.

The systems introduced are:

- affixation, that is suffixes and prefixes, and also 'zero affixes' (where a word moves from one class to another without changing its form, for example, **a change** and **to change**). This is also known as conversion.
- the formation of compound nouns.
- recognizing neutral, dramatic and formal style.

- homophones and homonyms.
- word-forms with shifting stress, for example, 'produce and pro'duce.
- compound adjectives
- multi-word verbs
- idiomatic expressions
- synonyms and antonyms
- collocation
- phrasal nouns

3 Introducing students to new words. This is done by means of matching exercises, gap filling, labelling diagrams, and referring to texts, and is practised in dialogues, discussions and listening.

Two points remain to be made on the subject of vocabulary. It is always worth having dictionaries available in the classroom as they are an invaluable resource for you and your students to consult at any stage of a lesson.

Finally, all the above are conscious strategies for learning vocabulary, but one of the most 'painless' and perhaps one of the most effective ways of acquiring new words is by reading as much as possible. This way, words appear in context, and assimilation will take place subconsciously. There is more below on encouraging reading.

Revision sections

These cover areas of the language that students should be familiar with at this level. Some deal with areas that always seem to pose problems, for example **have** as an auxiliary verb and a full verb, short answers, and **get**. Others cover areas that students will have encountered before but perhaps not consciously considered, for example exclamations, the negation of the verb of opinion in sentences such as *I don't think it'll rain*, and nouns that change meaning depending on whether they are countable or uncountable.

The Revision sections appear at the end of every unit, but are intended for use at any time. They could well be done at the beginning of a lesson as a 'warm-up'.

The Workbook

The Workbook consists of controlled exercises to revise the target language of each unit, vocabulary work, gap filling exercises and a preposition syllabus. There is a full answer key at the back. The Workbook is intended for use both in class and at home.

There is an extensive revision test at the end of every four units, which covers the input and some of the skills work of the previous units. The final revision test takes the form of some parts of the Cambridge First Certificate examination.

Fluency work

The Skills Development activities in each unit have two aims:

- To develop students' abilities and proficiency in the four language skills and their integrated use, and to equip students to use language outside the classroom.
- To introduce and practise the target language of the unit, showing it in a natural context.

In these activities, students' attention is on the achievement of the task, and not on the language required. Naturally the role of the teacher is different in such activities. The teacher should set them up so that students are motivated and know what they have to do, but should not interfere too much thereafter. An excess of attention to accuracy would stop the flow of such activities.

Many of the approaches to the skills work suggested can be transferred to supplementary material that you may wish to use, for example pyramid discussions, plus/minus/interest points to an argument, exploiting topic sentences, and jumbled paragraphs.

Reading and listening

Great attention has been attached in *Headway* to including a wide variety of text-types on topics that appeal to educated adults. The sources of the reading material include encyclopaedias, classical, modern and popular literature, quizzes both serious and

amusing, popular and professional magazines, and daily newspapers. The material in the listening developments is either an authentic interview (for example, Units 3, 7, 10, and 12), or a script recorded by actors based on an authentic interview.

Emphasis is placed on pre-comprehension tasks to motivate students to want to read/listen and to bring to the fore their prior knowledge of the subject. This encourages them to predict content and thus decide what they want to learn from the text. Comprehension check questions test global and detailed understanding, and questions in the 'What do you think?' section invite students to give their own opinions and reactions.

To a certain extent, students can be helped in their reading and listening with part-skill (or sub-skill) work and appropriate comprehension strategies. However, the main improvement will come with practice, the development of their linguistic knowledge generally, and the confidence that comes from successful encounters with texts. The reading syllabus includes:

- skimming and scanning
- summarizing
- inference
- exploiting topic sentences
- appreciating literature

The listening syllabus includes:

- gist listening
- listening for specific information
- note taking
- summarizing main points
- inference

Naturally, students at this level should be encouraged to practise their English outside class as much as possible. Ideally, this practice should include all four skills. They might enjoy watching films in English, and listening to the World Service, but one of the easiest, cheapest, and most convenient ways of practising, as well as being one of the most pleasurable, is reading. A tremendous amount of sub-conscious 'learning' is taking place as a student enjoys a book. Not only is grammar being consolidated and vocabulary acquired, but from many books the student can also learn something of the culture of the target language.

However, what a student reads does not matter as long as the activity is enjoyable. It could be a graded reader, but at the upper-intermediate level students should be ready to encounter authentic texts, and there is a great deal of satisfaction when a student has successfully completed a book of 'real' English literature. You might all opt to buy the same book, which students read at home and you all discuss in class. This has the advantage that you can set the activity up in class, giving some information about the author, setting compre-hension questions and generally monitoring students' progress. Alternatively, your school might have a library, in which case students could all choose different books and tell each other about what they have been reading. Whichever you decide, encourage reading as much as possible, and keep asking students not only how they are getting on, but *how they read*. Do they use dictionaries? How often? How quickly do they read? What do they do when they don't understand something? In the experience of the authors, the following books have interested students at this level:

Short stories
Any publishers' collections of modern short stories
Roald Dahl
Somerset Maugham

Novels
George Orwell (*1984*, and *Animal Farm*)
Aldous Huxley (*Brave New World*)
John Fowles (*The Collector*)
William Golding (*Lord of the Flies*)

Speaking
There are at least two activities per unit to encourage free speaking. The Discussion Point at the beginning of the unit launches the theme, and the Speaking activity, either a discussion or a roleplay, further exploits the theme and practises the target language in a freer, more creative way.

However, there are many other opportunities for free speaking in other sections of the unit. The pre-comprehension tasks often take the form of a discussion to be conducted in groups, with whole-class feedback afterwards to compare information, or a survey where all members of the class state their opinions on a subject and the information must be assessed. Also, many of the questions in the 'What do you think?' section could easily lead to a discussion, with students bringing in personal reactions and instances from events currently in the news.

Pairwork is encouraged as the medium for many activities, both accuracy work and fluency work, and this too is a form of 'free speaking'. Even though two students might be working on a grammatical exercise, they still need to do things like giving and seeking opinions, and asking for information. The importance of this in the development of the speaking skill should not be minimized.

It is assumed that the individual teacher will be able to judge exactly how much time to allocate to free speaking activities. There needs to be a fine balance here. On the one hand, students frequently ask for 'conversa-tion' in valuable class time, and their request is reasonable. On the other hand, roleplays can seem like games and not 'real work', which can lead to complaints that 'the teacher doesn't make us work hard'. The role of free speaking activities in the process of language acquisition is extremely important, and there is evidence to suggest that it is through speaking and listening for authentic reasons that both first and second languages are learned. It is also expected that the individual teachers will know best what interests their own students, and will select topics for discussion accordingly.

Naturally, the teacher should not interrupt to correct while these activities are in progress. Equally, he or she should not hesitate to take part or give personal opinions on a subject. The teacher is a person with opinions as well, not merely a manipulator of others!

Writing
Writing is perhaps the easiest language skill to neglect in the syllabus and the timetable. Several reasons can be suggested for this. Speaking (and hence listening) are often the skills given most prominence, and when this is the case there is a feeling that writing is a waste of valuable classroom time. Situations when a student genuinely needs to speak English are much easier to predict than occasions when they really might need to write, and your students' motivation and needs to write will vary greatly. Furthermore, good writing is not the written form of spoken language, but has its own styles, conventions, and disciplines. Whilst we can talk of 'free speaking activities', where attention is on the communication of the message rather than linguistic accuracy, we cannot talk about equivalent 'free writing activities'. The written language does not tolerate error. When speaking, students can conceal error, but when writing, they have committed themselves 'in black and white' with regard to what they think is correct English. In this way, writing diagnoses the state of a student's language very starkly. It is for these reasons, the Writing Development activities in the Student's Book are labelled accuracy-based, not fluency-based, in the Teaching Notes.

The writing syllabus in *Headway Upper-Intermediate* is largely independent of the language syllabus. That is, while the reading, listening, and speaking activities have the dual aims of revision of the target language and the development of the relevant skill, the writing activities have their own areas of input and practice. In each unit, one aspect (or sub-skill) of the writing skill is highlighted and practised, and there is then a suggestion for extended writing for students to do as homework. Examples of these aspects are:

- formal versus informal style
- conjunctions and prepositions of time
- joining contrasting ideas
- reporting conversations

In Unit 1 there is an introduction to proof-reading, as the ability to find and correct mistakes is very important in the writing skill. In Unit 2 of the Student's Book and the Workbook, there are explanations and exercises on word order, which causes students many problems in English. There are also exercises on different reasons for writing, for example:

- a biography
- an appraisal of a book or film
- presenting an argument
- describing for information and describing to sell

Introduction to teaching notes

The teaching notes are divided into three parts.

Aims of the unit

This section provides you with an overview of the unit, giving main priorities and showing you how the unit fits into the course as a whole.

Notes on the language input

This section provides an analysis of the target language at a deeper level than is found in the Grammar section, and points to the places where students commonly make mistakes.

Notes on the unit

This provides step-by-step instruction on all the activities, giving suggestions for lead-in and further exploitation, the rationale of the activity when necessary, and answers to all the exercises. Each activity is preceded by an indication of its overall aim (either accuracy or fluency), and then the specific aims, so that you will always know exactly what you are trying to achieve.

It is important that your students are aware of the way in which *Headway Upper-Intermediate* is organized, so that they are clear about what they are doing and can use the book as a resource, and also so that they can prepare in advance. Such preparation

is especially beneficial before an input lesson. Tell your students what the aim of the next input lesson will be and ask them to:

- look at the Contents page under Language Input, Structure, and Use.
- read the Language Review page.
- read the appropriate part of the Grammar section.
- look at some of the exercises in the Controlled Practice section.

The upper-intermediate level

Students at this level have already been learning English for a considerable time. Whether your group is monolingual or multilingual, it is worth remembering several factors:

- Their reasons for learning will differ. Some may be learning for professional or academic reasons, others because English is seen as a useful qualification.
- Their attitudes to learning English will differ. Some may be enthusiastic, enjoying the challenge and eager to learn about a new language and its culture. Others may resent having to spend time, money and energy on a task that they find difficult.
- Whatever your students' attitudes, learning a language takes longer than most people think, and there are no easy routes to mastery. There can be a lot of frustration, especially at this level, because of the apparent slow rate of progress. A common cry from students is 'Oh no! Not the Present Perfect/Past Continuous/reported speech again! We already do this ten times!' As a teacher, one has to sympathize. The problem is that learning to understand and use a language is not like memorizing a list of historical dates, and as the nineteenth-century educationalist von Humboldt said, 'We cannot teach a language. We can only create the conditions in which it is learned.'

- Their preferred learning styles will differ. Whether by educational background or individual opinion, your students will have different ideas about how best they like to learn, and hence how best you ought to teach! Some will expect a very rigid course, and resist pair and group work, wanting to hear only the teacher's voice; many students equate learning a language with learning the grammar, and do not see the point of activities such as roleplay in the classroom.

There is, of course, no way that you can reconcile or cater for all of the above! You have to try to please most of the people most of the time. Do find out, however, why your students are learning, and try to ascertain their attitude to the task. The aim of Unit 1 is very much to discuss attitudes and approaches to learning English, and hopes to make the point that there is no *one* way.

Bear in mind at all stages of the course what the theorists tell us are the characteristics of a good learner. He/she is:

- confident in his/her ability to learn
- self-reliant
- motivated and enthusiastic
- aware of why he/she wants to learn
- unafraid of making mistakes, and unafraid of what he/she doesn't know
- a good risk-taker
- a good guesser
- probably positive in his/her attitude to English language and culture
- a good pattern perceiver
- prepared to look for opportunities to come into contact with the language
- willing to assume a certain responsibility for his/her own learning

No student will possess all these virtues! This list is given for you to encourage your students as much as possible at every stage of the course. A student's motivation is, no doubt, the greatest factor affecting learning, but after that, it could be argued that the second greatest factor is the teacher's ability to maintain that motivation.

UNIT 1

The tense system

Languages and language learning

AIMS OF THE UNIT

- As you begin *Headway Upper-Intermediate*, you are probably beginning a new course, and possibly with a new group of students. Your main aim will be *introduction*, as you get to know your students and they get to know each other, and together you discuss the aims and priorities of the course to come.

- The aim of Unit 1 is also introduction. It encourages students to discuss their attitude to learning English so that they become more aware of the strategies they adopt. They should be able to compare and swap ideas with their colleagues. A factor which students should realize is that learning is an *active* process (see 'The characteristics of a good learner' on page vii of the Teacher's Book).

- More specifically, students are introduced to the English tense system, and to some of the systems of vocabulary (see page i of the Teacher's Book). They are encouraged to develop their own method of keeping vocabulary records and to proof-read their writing before it is marked.

- Notice that there is an Initial Test at the beginning of the Workbook for you to assess your students' general level of English. This test covers areas of the language that your students should be familiar with. You could set this for homework, or do it in class in the first day or two.

NOTES ON THE LANGUAGE INPUT

The tense system

The aim is again one of introduction. Many of the English tenses were presented in *Headway Intermediate*, and in this unit of *Headway Upper-Intermediate*, students are exposed to the remaining ones. The emphasis is on *recognition* rather than *production*, the idea being to provide students with a framework or overview of possible forms, and to stress the concepts that all continuous tenses have in common, and also those that all perfect tenses have in common. All of the tenses are dealt with in more depth in later units. English is often described as a rich language, and this is certainly true of its tense system. The simple/continuous distinction runs through the whole tense system, requiring the speaker or writer to decide whether the verb action should be viewed as a complete whole (simple tenses) or as an activity with duration (continuous tenses). This characteristic is not so pervasive in other languages; for example note the French, German, and Italian translations of the two English sentences below:

He works in a bank.
He's working in the garden.

French
Il travaille dans une banque.
Il travaille dans le jardin.

German
Er arbeitet in einer Bank.
Er arbeitet im Garten.

Italian
Lui lavora in una banca.
Lui lavora nel giardino.

Spanish can make this distinction:
Trabaja en un banco.
Está trabajando en el jardin.

However, Spanish and English uses of the continuous are not identical. Other Romance and Germanic languages have perfect tenses, which express similar concepts to English, but the distinction between Past Simple (for an action completed at a specific time) and the Present Perfect (for an action completed some time before now) causes students considerable difficulty. The Present Perfect in English expresses a way of viewing a past action in terms of its relation to the present that is not expressed by the verb in other languages:

I have seen him.
I saw him yesterday.

French
Je l'ai vu.
Je l'ai vu hier.

German
Ich habe ihn gesehen.
Ich habe ihn gestern gesehen.

Italian
L'ho visto.
L'ho visto ieri.

Again Spanish makes a distinction:
Le/lo he visto.
Le/lo vi ayer.

Students will, of course, have been exposed to both continuous and perfect tenses in their previous study of English. The aim here is to provide them with a view of the whole system, and to enable them to see the logic behind it.

NOTES ON THE UNIT

- Before beginning the unit, make sure students are familiar with the organization of the book. Each unit is divided into the following sections.

  - Discussion Point
  - Reading
  - Vocabulary 1
  - Vocabulary 2
  - Listening
  - Speaking
  - Writing
  - Language Review
  - Controlled Practice
  - Revision

You could ask questions such as 'Where is the contents page?', 'Where is the Grammar section?', 'Where is the tapescript for the listening on page 3?' 'Where is the Grammar section for Unit 3?' etc. Familiarity with the organization will enable students to perceive the aims of each activity and to participate as much as possible, as well as allowing them to revise from material already covered, and to prepare for lessons in advance.

● Discussion point

Aims

- fluency
- free speaking to launch the theme of languages and language learning.

- Introduction: have a short discussion on languages. Choose from the following questions, depending on your students.

  What difficulties do you think someone learning your language would have?
  Is it easy or difficult to learn?
  What do you know about the history of your language?
  How far back does the literature go?

What language group does it belong to?
How many languages do you speak? Are you bi-lingual?

- Students work in pairs or small groups to answer the seven questions in the Student's Book. Make sure they don't look at the answers on page 2! Let this go on for five minutes, or as long as students are interested. They might be able to deduce the answer to some of the questions, and they might say, quite rightly, that they have no idea of the answer to others. They could well ask what Esperanto is. Say 'an artificial language invented in the nineteenth century'.

- Students check their answers in the key.

  Use the answers as a basis for discussion. Your questions will depend on your students' interests and knowledge. Choose from the following.

  What is the population of China?
  Where is English spoken as a first language? As a second language?
  What do you know about life in ancient Egypt? What did people write on?
  What is the main language in India? (Hindi)
  Why should someone invent an artificial language?
  Where is Spanish spoken?

● Reading

Aims

- fluency
- to develop students' reading abilities
- to provide some background information about the English language.

- Introduction: students work in pairs to do the Pre-reading task. Let this go on for as long as students are interested, perhaps five minutes. Don't let students' enthusiasm for the topic flag. Remember this is just a warm-up for the reading.

- Students skim the text to get the answers to the true/false questions. You could set this as a competition

to ensure that students do in fact skim, by saying 'See who can find all the answers first'. It is very important that they practise the different ways of reading a text, either skimming quickly for gist, scanning quickly for certain information, or reading slowly for detailed comprehension.

Answers

1 False	5 True	
2 True	6 True	
3 False	7 False	
4 True		

- Students read the text more carefully, and answer the Comprehension Check/Language Work questions. These will test students' ability to form questions accurately.

Answers

1 *How many people spoke English in Shakespeare's time?*
2 *Why has English become a world language?*
3 *When did the exporting of English begin?*
4 *How much of the world's mail is in English?*
5 *How many of the world's telephone calls are in English?*
6 *Did Old English have inflections?*
7 *What are the basic characteristics of English?*
8 *Which language is spoken by most people?*

- Answer the 'What do you think?' questions as a class discussion.

Answers

1 The text comes from an encyclopaedia. It gives a general introduction to English, providing information about its history and its characteristics. Dictionaries provide information about *words* only. A brochure for an English language school would give information about courses, dates, and fees, and a preface to a book on modern language teaching would talk about teaching and learning different languages, not just English.

2 The text refers to the great growth of population in the

United States. Another reason, no doubt, is the economic importance of the United States, and its technological developments which are exported all over the world.

3 Your students will presumably belong to either the second or third group of English speakers. This is an interesting opportunity to find out and discuss students' reasons for learning, and their attitude to learning. Do they *want* to, or were they *forced* to?

4 You could prompt this by saying that about half the words in English have a Germanic origin, and half Romance, but English has borrowed widely e.g.

Arabic	*admiral*
Spanish	*mosquito, cigar*
Italian	*piano*
Hindi	*pyjamas*
Chinese	*tea*

Students should have little difficulty in thinking of borrowed words in their own language, both from English and other languages.

● Listening

Aims
– fluency
– to develop students' ability to distinguish between different English accents.

– Play the tape, and stop the cassette after each speaker, so that students can discuss their answers in pairs.

It is unlikely that they will be able to get all the answers correct by identifying the accents only. They might recognize the American accent and the British accent, but recognizing accents in a foreign language is generally quite difficult. They may have to rely on the large hints provided about the capital cities.

Answers

American	4	Welsh	6
Australian	1	Irish	2
Scottish	5	English	3

Language focus
Aims

– accuracy
– to introduce students to the tense system
– to introduce students to the continuous and perfect aspect
– to practise basic tenses, present, past, and future.

– Read the Language Review all together.
– Sentences for translation (see page iv of the Teacher's Book).
  I live in Rome.
  I'm living in London at the moment.
  She works in a bank.
  She's working in the garden at the moment.
  They lived in New York from 1960 to 1970.
  I've lived here all my life.
  Have you ever seen the Queen?
  I saw the Queen yesterday.
– Students study the Grammar section for homework.
– Do the Controlled Practice exercises.

Students do exercise 1 in pairs or small groups.

Even though students might not have been introduced to all the tense forms, they should have no great difficulty completing the tense charts. Their logic should guide them, they will have come across the forms in their reading, and their colleagues will help.

Continuous tenses are formed with the auxiliary verb **to be** + the present participle.

Perfect tenses are formed with the auxiliary verb **to have** + the past participle.

Passive tenses are formed with the auxiliary verb **to be** + the past participle.

– Students could well ask about the difference between certain tenses, or want to know the meaning of tenses that they are not familiar with. Without discouraging them, say that the *meaning* and *use* will be dealt with in later units, and that the aim of this exercise is to show students the possible *forms*.

Answers

ACTIVE	Simple	Continuous
Present	*he works*	*he's working*
Past	*he worked*	*he was working*
Future	*he will work*	*he will be working*
Present Perfect	*he has worked*	*he has been working*
Past Perfect	*he had worked*	*he had been working*
Future Perfect	*he will have worked*	

PASSIVE	Simple	Continuous
Present	*it is mended*	*it is being mended*
Past	*it was mended*	*it was being mended*
Future	*it will be mended*	
Present Perfect	*it has been mended*	
Past Perfect	*it had been mended*	
Future Perfect	*it will have been mended*	

- Students do exercise 2 in pairs.

Answers

has become – Present Perfect Simple (active)

began – Past Simple (active)

speak – Present Simple (active)

are forced – Present Simple (passive)

have been simplified – Present Perfect Simple (passive)

do not change – Present Simple (active)

have contributed – Present Perfect Simple (active)

is now being reversed – Present Continuous (passive)

are resisting – Present Continuous (active)

will die – Future Simple (active)

- Exercise 3 is a diagnostic test for you to see how good your students are with basic present, past, and future tenses. Ideas and tenses are cued, but there will naturally be mistakes. Don't attempt lengthy remedial teaching at this point, but prompt students for the correct answer, perhaps via peer correction. All tenses are dealt with in later units.

If this is the beginning of a new course, another aim is for people to get to know one another. If everybody already knows one another, it is a nice idea to invite someone into your class for students to ask their questions to. This could be any English speaker – for example a colleague, a friend, or a receptionist.

Students work in pairs to prepare their questions. This is a very important stage, and should be done very carefully. As the pairs are preparing, go round checking and correcting. Students should be familiar with the necessary tenses – Past Simple, Present Perfect, Present Simple and Continuous, **will** and **going to** – but expect varying degrees of accuracy.

Students ask you the questions first to check on accuracy (and to get to know you if they don't already),

then do exercise 4. Let this go on as long as the students are interested. It could well develop into a fluency activity, as they finish their prepared questions and are motivated to ask additional ones. This should be encouraged if you have time.

● Vocabulary 1

Aims

- accuracy
- to highlight and practise three of the basic characteristics of English mentioned in the article: flexibility of form, the creation of compounds, and the creation of derivatives with suffixes and prefixes.

- Students work in pairs to label the diagram.
Encourage them to ask for more words if they want.
Drill the items for pronunciation.

- Remind students of the way nouns can be used as verbs, e.g. **a swim**, **to swim**; **a drink**, **to drink**; **a kiss**, **to kiss**.
Students do exercise 2 in small groups.

This is an intriguing but quite difficult exercise. It may take students one or two examples to see that the verb required is a part of the body, and they may offer verbs such as **give** or **pass** in (a), and **kick** in (b). The aim of the exercise is not so much for students to learn the new words, or familiar words used as verbs, but to begin to see how English is a very flexible language.

Answers

a. *hand*   e. *fingered*
b. *headed*   f. *armed*
c. *backed*   g. *thumb*
d. *shoulder*

- Do the exercise on compounds all together.

Answers

a. *To keep their hair out of their eyes.*
b. *In New York.*
c. *Words such as 'Rest in peace', 'John Smith, 1940–1980'.*
d. *You're making progress.*

e. *Headlights.*
f. *Headlines.*
g. *You put on headphones.*

- Students work in pairs for five minutes to prepare their questions. As they are preparing, go round to check and correct. Encourage students to select useful words rather than obscure ones, and make sure questions are correctly formed.

- Do the exercise on derivatives quite quickly. Again, the aim is to show students part of the vocabulary system rather than explore a lot of words, and there has already been quite a lot of work on vocabulary. There is an exercise in Unit 1 of the Workbook which practises derivatives.

● Speaking

Aims

- fluency
- to discuss students' attitudes to language learning
- to make students aware of their own strategies for language learning
- to allow students to contribute their own ideas regarding the content and balance of your timetable.

- Students discuss question 1 either all together, or in groups.

- Students complete the boxes with their own ideas first, then compare in groups, then try to agree as a class. This is called a pyramid discussion. Although the aim is to come to a single conclusion, this is rarely possible, which is only natural.

In this exercise, you are getting students' opinions as to their expectations from the course. It can be very interesting to find out what these are. Because your presence might inhibit open discussion, a possible approach is for you to leave the room for five or ten minutes, telling students to appoint a spokesperson, and asking them to collate their opinions on the board. You then return and discuss their conclusions, comparing them with your own.

Although students' expectations should be considered, you should not feel that your own ideas must be compromised or dropped to 'keep the customer satisfied'. You, after all, should know more about teaching methodologies and devising a balanced timetable, and students can have some strange ideas about what constitutes language learning. But be prepared to discuss with students how you intend to structure the course and take into consideration their comments. They often say that they would like to be corrected all the time. Point out that this is not only impracticable but undesirable.

– Encourage students to contribute their own ideas for effective language learning. You could make the point that although teachers are important, the responsibility for learning is the students'. Discuss some of the ideas on 'The characteristics of a good learner' (page vii of the Teacher's Book).

● Listening

Aims

– fluency
– to develop students' listening abilities.

– Students do the pre-listening task in pairs or small groups. The aims are to bring to the fore what students already know about Esperanto, which might not be very much, and more especially, for students to decide what they would like to learn from the programme, i.e. they devise their own pre-set questions.

– Play the introduction to the programme, pausing after '. . . there are many who would like Esperanto to be the official second language of the world'. Students answer question 1 in pairs.

– Play the rest of the tape twice, while students fill in the charts.

Answers

Advantages of Esperanto:
People from different countries could talk to each other easily, about all sorts of subjects.
Translation costs would be reduced.
It is a neutral language, so everybody would be equal in having to learn it.
It is easy to learn; there are no exceptions.
People learn it very quickly.

Disadvantages of English:
Many people resent having to learn it.
English is not an easy language to learn.
English has problems of spelling, there are many exceptions to rules, and it is very idiomatic. It seems easy in the beginning, but takes a long time to master. There are difficulties in pronunciation because there are so many vowel sounds.

– Answer the 'What do you think?' questions 1 and 2 as a class.

– Students work in groups to answer question 3. Then take a vote to answer question 4.

● Vocabulary 2

Aims

– accuracy
– to help students decide how best to keep vocabulary records.

– There is no task to this section of Unit 1. Read and discuss it together. Probably only the most conscientious students will have decided how they keep vocabulary records. For the rest you should stress the importance of doing *something* with the words they meet.

– The minimum a student should do is have a special vocabulary notebook, where words are recorded with their part of speech, a note on stress, and with some attempt to illustrate meaning which might take the form of a sentence containing the item, a definition, or a translation. The more assiduous will adopt some or all of the suggested approaches, but this requires a considerable degree of application.

– You could adopt several of the following ideas:

Ask students in the next lesson if they have bought a special notebook, and if so, ask them how they intend to organize it.

Check their notebooks regularly, and ask them what they do to add to them and revise from them.

Make sure that when you are doing vocabulary work in class, students make records in their vocabulary notebooks.

Set as occasional homework the task of reading something in English, and looking up and learning a certain number of words, perhaps between five and ten.

Introduce students to 'spidergraphs' as a way of brainstorming vocabulary. You could provide the topic and the 'branches', and leave it to students to complete it with whatever words they want.

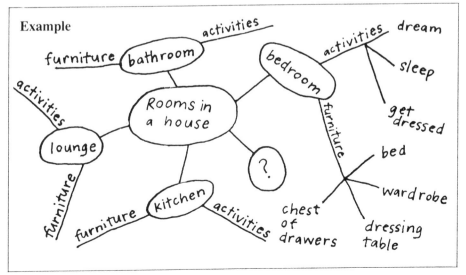

Example

5

Spidergraphs are also useful for brainstorming vocabulary related to ways of doing things; for example, cooking, walking, speaking, travelling.

Example

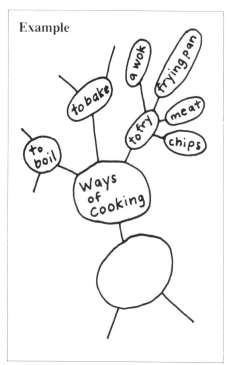

(spidergraph)
- to bake
- a wok
- frying pan
- to fry
- meat
- chips
- to boil
- Ways of cooking

● Writing

Aims

- accuracy
- to give practice in proof-reading, so students can carefully check their written homework before handing it in
- to introduce students to the kinds of symbols you will use when correcting their homework.

- Read the introduction together, making sure they understand the symbols.
- Students first try to correct the mistakes on their own, then check with a colleague.

Answers

/   a. My friend ~~she~~ came to see me last night.

Wo   b. I am going to the village where (live) my parents.

/ Sp   c. He told ~~to~~ me a story, wich [h] was very funny.

/ /   d. When I arrived ~~to~~ home, I had ~~the~~ dinner.

Gr P   e. She speaks ~~e~~nglish [E], ~~f~~rench [F] and ~~r~~ussian [R].

P   f. The dog broke it's leg.

/ Sp   g. He gave ~~to~~ me a pen for my bi[r]thday.

∧   h. She's [a] doctor.

T   i. She's [has been] a doctor for five years.

∧ Wo   j. I explained [to] the teacher why (was) I late.

/ Gr   k. ~~The~~ American people [are] ~~is~~ very generous.

WW Sp   l. I ~~made~~ [did] my homework very careful[l]y.

- Students correct the composition in the same way.

Answers

∧ WW

∧ /

T

∧

Wo T

Sp

WW Wo
   WW

T

WW Sp

WW Gr

WW

P

T

My name is Luis Gonzalez, and I come from Mexico. I [was] born in 1951 in ~~one~~ [a] small village outside Mexico City. When I was six years [old] I went to ~~the~~ nursery school, and I enjoyed it very much. When I was eleven I~~////~~ moved to Brazil, because my father is [a] diplomat, so ✓my (all) life I [have] lived in different~~y~~ countries. After school, I [went] ~~was~~ (for four years) ~~in~~ [to] a business college↓ and I got a degree in business administration. I['m] working for a company that products [produces] small calculators.It's a good ~~work~~ [job], and I'm very interesting [ed] ~~for~~ [in] computers. I want to learn ~~e~~nglish [E] because my father and I ~~will~~ [are going to] start our own business in America soon.

- Students write a composition about themselves for homework. Note that they are being tested in basic present, past, and future tenses, so this exercise has a diagnostic purpose in the same way as the Controlled Practice exercises 3 and 4.

  It is also an opportunity for you to learn something about the individual members of your class if you do not already know them.

- It is an extremely useful exercise for students to swap written work and try to correct it (in pencil) before handing it in to you to correct.

REVISION

Aims

- accuracy
- to give students practice in recognizing and producing numbers and dates.

- This is a very straightforward area, but one where students constantly make mistakes of form and pronunciation.

  Read 1 on dates together, then students work in pairs to practise the dates in exercise 2. After a while, ask one or two students to read them out aloud.

- Read 1 on numbers together.

- Students do the dictation on their own. Make sure they understand that they only have to write the numbers, not the words, i.e. that they should not *spell* the numbers.

  Play the tape once, then let students compare with a colleague. Play the tape again for students to check.

Answers

1 *182*	9 *8.7%*
2 *7.20*	10 *5½%*
3 *409*	11 *£27.50*
4 *¾*	12 *£5,500*
5 *12,000*	13 *0106 744391*
6 *150*	14 *3,649,712*
7 *106*	15 *14.5%*
8 *672*	16 *260,000*

- The tape tests students' ability to *recognize* numbers. The remaining exercises test students' *productive* abilities.

- Among other difficulties they encounter, students often find it hard to distinguish between **thirteen** and **thirty**, **fourteen** and **forty** etc. This problem is connected with pronunciation of sounds and word stress.

  With numbers like **thirty** and **forty** the stress is always on the first syllable; but with numbers like **thirteen** and **fourteen**, the stress shifts according to the context.

Example

I've got 'fourteen books.
Stress on the first syllable when the number is followed by a noun.

I've got four'teen.
Stress on the second syllable when the number stands alone.

- Students do exercise 3 in pairs. After a while, ask one or two students to read aloud.

- Do exercise 4 all together.

UNIT 2

Present Perfect Simple and Continuous

The seven ages of man

AIMS OF THE UNIT

- The main aim of this unit is to help students with one of the most problematic tenses in English, the Present Perfect. Students will already have done a lot of work on this, but will probably still be making mistakes. The problem stems from the fact that the Present Perfect in English represents a way of looking at a past event and expressing its relationship with the present which is not realizable in many other languages. Exercises on the Present Perfect Simple are cued after the Shakespeare extract and the reading 'Allen is a little disaster'; exercises on the Present Perfect Continuous are cued after the reading 'Allen is a little disaster' and after the listening about the audition.

- Vocabulary 2 concentrates on helping students to guess the meaning of unknown words, by exploiting linguistic and contextual clues.

- The theme of acting and the theatre runs through the unit. This could easily be expanded on with supplementary skills work and vocabulary.

NOTES ON THE LANGUAGE INPUT

Present Perfect Simple and Continuous

Much has already been written on the perfect aspect, and the problems that a foreign learner faces with the use of the Present Perfect in English. See *Headway Intermediate*, Teacher's Book and Student's Book, and *Headway Upper-Intermediate*, Teacher's Book page iii–iv and Student's Book pages 16 and 111.

In many European languages there are tenses which are formed in the same way as the Present Perfect in English, that is, the auxiliary verb **have** + the past participle, but they are not always used in the same way. Students need to appreciate that the use of the Present Perfect is governed not only by the *time* of the verb action, but by the way that the speaker/writer views the verb action.

This unit approaches the problem analytically and comprehensively, comparing and contrasting not only the Present Perfect and the Past Simple, but also the Present Perfect Simple and the Present Perfect Continuous.

NOTES ON THE UNIT
 Discussion point

Aims

- fluency
- free speaking to launch the theme of 'the seven ages of man'.

- Students work in pairs to put ages next to the people. There are no set answers here, except that the teenage years by definition last from 13 to 19. Adulthood might be said to begin at 18 or 21 – some might argue that it is to do with maturity

rather than a prescribed age – and lasts for the rest of one's life. Younger students have some alarming ideas regarding when old age begins, seeing life in general decline after 30!

- The three questions below this exercise could easily form the basis of a long and rewarding discussion, if you have the time and if it fits your timetable. The topic is of universal interest, and everyone should have something to contribute.

The questions could be answered in groups if you think your students would be inhibited in a class discussion. However, what students have to say is generally so interesting that it is nice for everyone to be able to hear and comment on their colleagues' observations. Naturally, you will need to prompt with questions, e.g.:

What's good about being a baby?
When do they learn to walk and talk?
Do you think babies are frustrated that they can't talk?
People say that childhood is a time of innocence. Why?
What has a child learned to do by the time he or she is 2? 3? 5? 10?
What don't children like doing?
Why are the teenage years difficult for both the child and the parents?
What are the responsibilities that an adult has to shoulder?
'Life begins at 40.' What do you understand by this?
How old are the current world leaders?

- Ask similar questions to promote discussion about whether students are happy with their present age (*Were you happier when you were younger? What do you look forward to or fear in the next 'age'?*), but remember to be sensitive to students' feelings. The topic is of quite a personal nature, and a student might resent being probed too much.

Vocabulary 1

Aims

- accuracy
- Students practise using dictionaries and understanding definitions
- Students discuss the vocabulary in pairs.

- The vocabulary is a random selection of nouns, verbs, and adjectives that could easily be associated with a particular age. There is not necessarily always one correct answer. **A pension** is logically associated with old age, but **being ambitious** could be any age from teenage onwards.

It is very important that students do this exercise in pairs, and discuss their answers together. This will provide a quiet hum of activity for about twenty minutes. If students work alone there could be a rather heavy silence, and they might wonder why this activity is being done in class time.

It is interesting for you to look up words in the dictionary at the same time as your students. This will give you an idea of how long it takes, and you might be able to anticipate some of the problems they encounter.

Reading

Aims

- fluency
- to develop students' appreciation of a piece of classic literature.

- It is anticipated that students will find the text quite challenging, as there are several archaic or obscure

words. However, the Discussion Point and the Vocabulary should have warmed students to the theme; and the motivation to read some Shakespeare, and the satisfaction of understanding it, should be considerable. Students are by no means expected to understand every word. The glossary is intended to enable them to grasp the essential messages of the extract.

- Students first listen to the speech without reading it, and try to find the seven ages that Jaques describes.

Answers

infant
school-boy
lover
soldier
justice (judge)
old man
very old man

- Students read the text, listening either to you reading aloud or the tape, and stopping to consult the glossary. Do this quite thoroughly, so that students can begin to appreciate the extract.
You could then read the text aloud or play the tape again.
- Answer the Comprehension Check questions 1–3 all together as a class, to make sure that students have grasped the main points. In pairs they could become confused and dispirited.

Answers

1 Actors

2 **Exits and entrances** are when an actor comes onto the stage, or leaves it. In a person's life, they are birth and death.
Parts are the roles an actor plays. In a person's life, they could be several things – the way we are different as we grow up; the way we are different depending on who we are with (child, parent, colleague, superior etc.); the way our character changes.
Acts are the divisions of a play. In a person's life, they are the seven ages.

3 No, because it cries and is sick. He doesn't want to go to school.

He is singing a ballad.
He is violent and quick-tempered, but *looking for reputation in the mouth of a cannon* is not very clever.
He likes eating.
He's over 60.
He can't see or taste, and he probably can't remember or eat much.

- Students do question 4 in pairs. They should feel confident enough by now to answer the questions.

Answers

the school-boy	*the very old man*
the soldier	*the lover*
the old man	*the justice* (judge)
the infant	

- Do questions 5 and 6 all together.

Answers

5 He is making fun of the lover, who is young and rather immature. Ballads are usually addressed to qualities and features that could be termed attractive; for example, hair, voice, eyes, kindness.

6 Reputation might appear very attractive, but it doesn't last very long. Like a bubble, it soon disappears.

- Answer the 'What do you think?' questions all together.
The second question could be set as homework, with a prompt from you.

Example

Babies can be very interesting to watch as they grow up, and we can rediscover life through the eyes of a child. Children are very energetic and enthusiastic, and . . .

Language focus

Aims

- accuracy
- to help students understand the indefinite nature of the Present Perfect
- to analyze the difference between the Present Perfect and the Simple Past, and to provide controlled practice in the two tenses.

- Read the Language Review all together.
- Sentences for translation (see page iv of the Teacher's Book).

  I live in Paris.
  I've lived here for ten years. (unfinished past)
  I lived in New York before I came here.
  He has never seen a Shakespeare play. (experience)
  She saw Hamlet *yesterday.*
  I've lost my wallet. (present result of past event)
  I lost it last night.

- The Grammar section could be read for homework or in class. It is not very long.
- Do the Controlled Practice exercises.

  Students do exercises 1 and 2 in pairs or small groups. The questions about Shakespeare are all in the Past Simple; the questions about Jeffrey Archer use both the Past Simple and the Present Perfect.

- Students do exercise 3 in pairs. The aim is for further controlled practice of the two tenses, but in a more realistic context.

  It might be useful for the 'generals' etc. to prepare together, and also the 'journalists' who are going to interview them; similarly the other characters, and the 'journalists' who are going to interview them. After a while, bring the pairs together to conduct the interview. Preparing together in this way usually leads to more ideas and greater accuracy.

- When students have finished, you could ask one or two of the pairs to re-enact their interview, and this could be recorded for intensive correction.

● Vocabulary 2

Aims

- accuracy
- to give students guidance in ways of guessing the meaning of unknown words, using linguistic and contextual clues
- to introduce students to prefixes and suffixes which add a new meaning.

- Read the introduction and part 1 all together.
- Students do exercise 2 in small groups.

Answers

a. *not*
b. *opposite*
c. *not, or get something wrong;* e.g. *misinform, misdirect*
d. *too much*
e. *not enough*
f. *again*
g. *former*
h. *female*
i. *without*
j. *full of; having the quality of*
k. *opposed to; against*
l. *of oneself; without help* e.g. *automatic*
m. *supporting, in favour of*
n. *negative, reverse, opposite*
o. *small*
p. *after*
q. *before*

- Read part 3 all together.
  The aim of this kind of work is to show students that it *is* possible to guess the meaning of unknown words (although perhaps not with complete accuracy), and to instil a certain amount of confidence in doing this. However, your expectations should not be unrealistic, and there will still be many occasions when students are unable to deduce the meaning. Students do exercise 4 in pairs or small groups.
- Go round the groups to help and monitor. Be prepared to 'nudge' students if they give up too easily.

Example

cracked
- Did the swimming pool have water in it?
  What can you do to your head if you bang it against something hard?

penknife
- Can you see that there are two words?
  Do you know them both?

chopped off
- What accident could the boy cause to his finger with a knife?
  What idea does **off** often express?

Dettol
- Look at the headline for a definition.

- There is a different kind of exercise on guessing meaning in the Workbook.

Language focus

Aims

- accuracy
- to provide students with further controlled practice of the Present Perfect Simple and Past Simple
- to test students' understanding of the difference between the Present Perfect Simple and the Present Perfect Continuous.

- The reading text about Allen is further exploited for accuracy work, because it contains some interesting examples of the Present Perfect Simple and Continuous, and because students need as much consolidation of these two tenses as possible.
- Students do exercise 1 in pairs.

Answers

Present Perfect Simple
has cracked
has chopped . . . off
has made
has been
has raised
hasn't stopped
has been taken
has known
has got (Present Perfect in form, but present in meaning)
have also had

Present Perfect Continuous
has been going
have you been doing

Only the last example is interchangeable. *What have you done this time?* is possible. The other examples must stay in the same tense.

- Students do exercise 2 in pairs, or it could be done as a class activity. The latter has the advantage that you have greater control over the accuracy of what students say, and can correct intensively. Also, people are naturally curious about other people's accidents and their causes!

- Students do exercise 3 in pairs. Notice that, as it says in the Grammar section, English tends to use the Present Perfect Continuous if possible.

Answers
a. *have you known*
b. *have you been learning*
c. *have you learned*
d. *have you been working* (job)
e. *have you been living* (place)
f. *have you had . . . for*
g. *have you seen*

Students are likely to have some problems with this exercise. This area of grammar is complex and not easily explained, and the exercise confronts the problem directly. If necessary, tell students that more work on the Present Perfect Simple and Continuous is coming soon.

- Do exercise 4 all together.

The reason the tenses change is because of *aspect*. **Has chopped** is one of the many accidents in Allen's life, and is the 'experience' use of the Present Perfect; **chopped** is in the Past Simple because his mother lists Allen's accidents in chronological order since the age of one, and tells us *when* this particular accident happened. **Has raised** is the 'present result' use of the Present Perfect, used for giving news about recent events; **raised** is in the Past Simple because the writer now sees the verb action as a past event.

● Listening

Aims

- fluency
- to develop students' abilities in listening for information.

- Introduction: ask students if they have read any of Charles Dickens' novels, what sort of novels they are, and what the characters in his books are like.
- Read the introduction together. Ask students in pairs to look at the picture of Mr Micawber and the photos of the three actors, and decide which actor looks best for the part.

- Check students understand **audition**, and ask them what happens at an audition. What are the producer and director looking for?
- Students listen to the interview and fill in the chart. After the first listening, students should compare notes with a colleague. Then play the tape again to check.

Answers

Bill Frindall
+ Good actor, auditioned well. Right voice, caught the comic side of Mr Micawber, got the character right.
He has done a lot of work in the theatre, and not much television, so he has a lot of experience of playing character parts.
Right age.
− Not reliable, he has had a drink problem.
He has been out of work for about nine months.
He forgot some of his lines.

Harry Lime
+ Best of the actors.
He said his lines very confidently, he sounded the part, perhaps because he has just written a book on Dickens. He has a lot of experience on the stage and television.
He has been with the Royal Shakespeare Company for years.
− He doesn't look the part, too young and too tall.
People won't see him as Mr Micawber.

Victor O'Brian
+ Right age, right face. Auditioned well.
A funny man.
Very enthusiastic, he has been trying to get away from situation comedy roles.
− His face is too well-known, he has done a lot of situation comedy, not character parts.
He plays himself − could he adapt?

Students are not expected to write down all the information.

Language focus
Aims

- accuracy
- to analyze the difference between the Present Perfect Simple and the Past Simple, and the difference between the Present Perfect Simple and the Present Perfect Continuous.

- Students look at the tapescript of the audition and find the examples of the Present Perfect Simple and Continuous.

Answers
it's given us more problems than it's taken away.
everything's gone wrong . . .
he's had a lot of experience in character parts, . . .
it's all been in the theatre, hasn't it, . . .
What's he been doing recently?
Has he been in much?
He's been out of work for about nine months, . . .
Hasn't he just written a book on Dickens, or something?
he's got so much experience . . . (Present Perfect *form*, but present *meaning*)
He's been with the Royal Shakespeare Company for years, . . .
He's been trying to break away . . .

- Sentences for translation (see page iv of the Teacher's Book).
I work in London.
I've been working here for five years.
Before that I worked in America.
You look tired. What have you been doing?
I've been cleaning the house.
I cleaned it last week too.

- Do the Controlled Practice exercises in pairs, then check all together. Remember that these exercises confront a difficult area of grammar, and you cannot expect to 'teach' it easily. Students may feel frustrated as they attempt to understand the perfect and the continuous aspects, and they need to develop a 'feel' or an 'ear' for them.

Answers

4 a. In the first sentence, she no longer lives in New York. In the second, she does.

b. In the first sentence, there is the suggestion that the husband is dead. In the second he is still alive, and still buying flowers.

c. In the first sentence, the question asks about 'any time in your life'. The second question asks about a specific time in the past.

d. In the first sentence, the novel is finished. In the second, the novel is not finished.

e. The first question asks how many years you have been smoking, how long the activity has been going on. The second question wants to know the exact number of cigarettes that have been smoked today – ten cigarettes cannot 'continue to be smoked', they are finished.

f. The first question wants to know the action that led to the red eye. The second question wants to know all the different activities that the person has been engaged in.

5 a. The second sentence is wrong. If the exact time is given (last year) the Present Perfect cannot be used.

b. The second sentence is wrong. The word *first* suggests that the job in the factory has finished.

c. The first sentence is wrong. The event happened too long ago to be considered recent news.

d. The second sentence is wrong. The suggestion is horrible – that the action happened again and again. However, we can say 'He's been cutting wood'.

e. The first sentence is wrong. The continuous suggests that only part of the sandwich has been eaten, but the sandwich has all gone.

f. The second sentence is wrong. The continuous cannot be used when the object of the verb has a quantity or a number.

– There are more exercises on the Present Perfect in the Workbook.

● Speaking

Aims

– fluency
– to provide students with two opportunities for free speaking practice, in the discussion and then the roleplay.

– Students work in groups of four to decide who they think should get the part, and why. Let this go on for as long as students are interested.
– Students work in groups of three in the roleplay. Although the topic is quite serious, students will probably treat it in quite a light-hearted manner. Try to encourage students A and B to be tactful.

● Writing

Aims

– accuracy
– to provide students with some guidance on word order
– to provide students with the opportunity to further practise the Present Perfect in the biography writing.

– It is often said that word order in English is relatively fixed. In spoken English, sentence stress is used for emphasis where other languages highlight by means of word order. In written work, however, students make many mistakes of word order, as they transfer from their own language.
– Read the introduction all together.
– Students do exercises 1 and 2 in pairs.

Answers

1 a. *I always get the same presents at Christmas.*

b. *My aunt Freda sends me a pair of socks.*

c. *Last year I got ten pairs of socks from my relatives.*

d. *I like reading very much.*

e. *I don't know why somebody doesn't buy me a book.*

f. *I often used to read a book in bed before going to sleep.*

2 a. *My sister was born in Leicester in 1951.*

b. *She studied English literature at Newcastle University from 1967 to 1970.*

c. *She has worked as a lecturer at Oxford Polytechnic since 1974.*

d. *In 1980 something rather interesting happened to her.* (Or *Something rather interesting . . . in 1980.*)

e. *She swapped jobs and houses with a lecturer from a New York university for a year.*

– Students write a biography for homework.
– There is another exercise on word order with verbs that take direct and indirect objects in the Workbook, Unit 2.

REVISION

Aims

– accuracy
– to give students practice in recognizing and producing the letters of the alphabet.

– Even at this level, students can make mistakes with the letters that are easily confused with their own language, e.g. *a e i j g r*. It is also difficult for them to copy down letters dictated at speed, and to say letters at speed, as there is a lot of catenation (joining of sounds).
– Students do exercise 1 in pairs.

Answers

1	2	3	4	5	6	7
a	b	f	i	o	q	r
h	c	l	y		u	
j	d	m			w	
k	e	n				
	g	s				
	p	x				
	t	z				
	v					

Students can practise the letters going down the columns, and by testing each other, one student pointing to a letter for the other to pronounce.

- Students do the dictation on their own. Play the tape once, then let students check in pairs. Play the tape again. Students can look at the tapescript to confirm their answers.

- Read part 3 all together.

- Before doing exercise 4, ask all the students to write down their name and address, and decide where they will break up the letters, and where the vowel sound links are.
  They then work in pairs to dictate their name and address. Stress that they should do it with speed and rhythm.

- Exercises 5 and 6 are fun activities, but quite important to get right.

Answers

5 *Jane* (g)   *Atkins* (s)
   Tracy (g)   *James* (b s)
   Frances (g)   *Green* (s)
   Jean (g)   *Ellis* (s)
   Pat (g b)   *Wilmot* (s)
   Joe (b)   *Hughes* (s)
   Graham (b s)   *Joyce* (g s)
   Terry (b s)   *Robson* (s)
   Joan (g)   *Alan* (b)

6 Prime Minister
   Bachelor of Arts
   Member of Parliament
   Bachelor of Science
   British Broadcasting Corporation
   Doctor of Philosophy
   European Economic Community
   Unidentified Flying Object
   répondez s'il vous plaît (please
      reply)
   Please Turn Over
   Value Added Tax
   miles per hour
   United Nations Organization
   postscript
   exempli gratia (for example)
   id est (that is)

UNIT 3

Verb patterns

Work

AIMS OF THE UNIT

- The topic of work is explored in the skills work and the vocabulary.
- The wide-reaching area of gerunds and infinitives is dealt with in the language input.
- There is a challenging reading text designed to match people to jobs scientifically, and an entertaining speaking activity which leads to much friendly argument.
- The style of formal letters is examined.

NOTES ON THE LANGUAGE INPUT

Gerunds and infinitives

Gerunds and infinitives occur frequently in English. They cause few problems of meaning, except where both are possible after a verb (for example, **stop**, **remember**, **try**), but students often make mistakes of form.

Common mistakes

After get up, I had a bath.
I want go home.
The sun stopped to shine.
I'm looking forward to meet you.
I came here for learning English.
He wanted that I helped him.

NB *Incorrect forms are indicated here, and elsewhere in the Teacher's Book, by asterisks.*

Notice particularly this last mistake. In many languages, this concept is

expressed by **want** + **that** + person + verb. In English it is expressed by **want** + direct object + infinitive.

NOTES ON THE UNIT
● Discussion point

Aims

- fluency
- free speaking to launch the theme of work
- to introduce some English proverbs.

- Students work in groups of four to complete the proverbs. They should be encouraged to use their logic and their dictionaries.

- The introduction to the *Oxford Advanced Learner's Dictionary of Current English* has an interesting paragraph on proverbs.

Answers

A bad workman blames his tools.
If a job is worth doing, it's worth doing well.
Make hay while the sun shines.
Many hands make light work.
Too many cooks spoil the broth.
Early to bed and early to rise makes you healthy, wealthy, and wise.
Never put off till tomorrow what you can do today.
The devil makes work for idle hands.
All work and no play makes Jack a dull boy.
The early bird catches the worm.

Make sure students understand all the vocabulary, and the message of the proverbs.

- The discussion on the truth value of proverbs, and proverbs from other languages can be entertaining and informative. Proverbs can be very similar, but sometimes a

Proverbs   You should note that *proverbs* are seldom used in ordinary speech or writing. Although the native speaker knows the meaning of most English proverbs, he will actually use one rarely, and then only when he is wanting to be humorous, or by referring to the proverb in an indirect way (for example by quoting only half of it), or by introducing it by saying something like 'You know what they say, . . .' or 'As the old saying goes, . . .' The reason is this. English proverbs are phrases or sentences containing advice, warning or truth. Although they are expressed in striking language, in their meanings they are rather obvious remarks to make about human experience. They are thought of as the sort of remark that would be made by someone who is rather dull, someone who cannot express in his own words what he thinks or feels, but who has to borrow a proverb from the language to do this. A *proverb*, a *cliché*, a *truism*, a *hackneyed phrase*, and a *trite remark* are all the sorts of expressions that someone who wants to express himself clearly, carefully and honestly will try to avoid.

language group comes up with one that even when translated and explained means very little to the rest of the class!

● Vocabulary 1

Aims

- accuracy
- to introduce students to a set of vocabulary relating to work
- to encourage students to perceive conceptual relationships between words
- to act as an introduction to the reading text which follows.

- It is important that students work in pairs or small groups to do this exercise. Interaction with peers, discussing the meaning of the words, and deciding which category to put them in are the essence of the activity.
There is not necessarily only one answer. Students could justify placing an item in several categories.
- Students work alone to write a description of a profession. As they are writing, go round helping and correcting.
- Students read out their descriptions for the others to guess what the profession is.

● Reading

Aims

- fluency
- to develop students' reading abilities
- to practise intensive reading.

- The sixty-four questions might look a little daunting, but the quiz does not in fact take too long to do. People generally find quizzes attractive, as they tell us something about ourselves. This is a scientifically-devised quiz, and finding out whether we are in the right profession, or which profession we should pursue, is a highly motivating subject.
- Do the pre-reading task all together. Students might wonder

which professions fit under 'People' and which under 'Procedures and Systems', but this doesn't matter, as they will find out at the end.

- Do the quiz all together. This will ensure that all the students understand all the questions. If students do it on their own at their own speed, you will probably find yourself explaining the same problem again and again as different students get to it! Some of the questions are a little tricky, especially those with a *negative* in them.

Example

Insults don't worry me. If insults *do* worry you, you have to circle False.

- Go through all the questions very carefully, adding up the scores at the end of each section and then the final scores.
- Read the interpretation all together, then let students read the section where they scored highest.
- Answer the first 'What do you think?' question all together, then question 2 in pairs or small groups.

Answers

I always help a colleague who has family problems, and *Other people's problems don't interest me.*

In a new group of people I often feel anxious, and *I feel comfortable in nearly all social situations.*

I find it hard to express myself in groups, and *I sometimes find it difficult to say what I mean.*

Personal insults don't worry me, and *Other people's comments about me don't hurt me.*

I always try to finish what I start, and *I don't always finish what I begin.*

If someone upsets me, I tell them that they have, and *I don't try to hide my emotions.*

- Answer questions 3 and 4 all together. There are no prescribed answers, so if you have a quiet

class you might have to prompt with questions.

Example

Does a nurse/doctor/teacher/ engineer have to be able to express himself/herself?

Does a gardener/artist/electrician/ banker/computer programmer have to be ambitious? etc.

- Students answer question 5 in groups. This can lead to a very fruitful discussion.

Language focus

Aims

- accuracy
- to provide students with controlled practice of gerunds after prepositions, verbs, and as the subject of a sentence; and controlled practice of infinitives after certain adjectives and verbs.

- Read the Language Review all together.

- Sentences for translation (see page iv of the Teacher's Book).
After getting up, I had a bath.
She left the room without saying anything.
I like working with my hands.
Smoking is dangerous.
Translating foreign languages is difficult.
I always try to finish what I start.
I want you to help me.
I came here to learn English.

- Students read the Grammar section for homework.

- Do the Controlled Practice exercises.
Students do exercises 1−3 in pairs or small groups. There are no set answers. Make sure that their answers are not only grammatically correct but that they make sense. *I have difficulty in looking out of the window*, for example, is nonsense.

- As an introduction to the listening, ask students how bread is made, then ask how flour is made.

Students listen to the interview and make sentences. After they have been working for a few minutes, play the tape again to refresh their memories.

Sample answers

a. *He didn't enjoy living in London.*
b. *He couldn't afford to give up work entirely.*
c. *He had always been interested in playing with engines and motors.*
d. *He and his wife decided to buy a windmill.*
e. *He managed to repair the windmill.*
f. *He finished repairing it before Christmas last year.*
g. *They were thinking of buying another mill.*
h. *They decided not to buy another mill.*
i. *He doesn't regret leaving his well-paid job.*
j. *They prefer living in the country to living in the town.*
k. *At first the boys weren't used to living in a small village.*

● Vocabulary 2

Aims

- accuracy
- to introduce students to a set of vocabulary, i.e. adjectives to describe character.

- Abstract concepts can be very difficult to teach. Although some of the items are straightforward, care needs to be taken. It is not always the case that a characteristic is purely positive or purely negative − for example, being **frank** is not always the best policy, and **proud** has two meanings, one positive and one negative.

Answers

helpful *I always help a colleague who has family problems.*
insecure *In a new group of people I often feel anxious.*
proud *I enjoy telling other people about my achievements.*

competitive *I always like to win when I take part in an activity.*
frank *If someone upsets me, I tell them that they have.*
organized *I like to keep things in order.*
conventional *Traditional solutions are the best.*
self-centred *Other people's problems don't interest me.*
cautious *I like to predict results before beginning to do anything.*
careless *Checking detail is not one of my strong points.*
thorough *I always try to finish what I start.*

- Most of the other statements under 'People' and 'Procedures and Systems' lend themselves to an adjective, but not all.

Example

considerate *I always think of other people's opinions . . .*
mathematical *I like working with statistics.*
forgetful *I frequently forget where I leave things.*
_____ *I cannot often persuade others.*
_____ *Personal insults don't worry me.*

Words that should come out are: **impressionable, ambitious, energetic, unreliable, self-confident, logical, shy/inarticulate.**

● Speaking

Aims

- fluency
- to provide students with an opportunity for free speaking practice
- to practise the skills of negotiating and giving opinions.

- This kind of activity is much used in management training. Students are presented with a problem and a 'menu' of choices. They have to discuss, negotiate, argue, and persuade until they reach a group decision. They are then presented with the 'result' of their decision, another problem and another 'menu' of choices. This continues until they are out of the maze.

- Students invariably find such activities extremely absorbing and entertaining. As they are working in groups, they come up against many differences of opinion, and much lively debate ensues. Although the topic of the maze is serious, many of the problems and choices are very amusing. The activity lasts between thirty minutes and an hour. If students are slow to make decisions, or cannot 'get out of the maze', they don't finish at all! Often when a group reaches Situation 22, and are given the choice of stopping or going back and trying again, they choose the latter.

- You can find Situation 1 in the Student's Book. Situations 2 to 22 are published here in the Teacher's Book for you to photocopy. You will need a complete set of the situations for each group of four in your class − so if you have twelve students, you will need three complete sets. We suggest you make the copies, cut out the individual situations, and stick them onto card so that they are easily re-usable. An additional suggestion is to stick the different sets onto different coloured card. If you do this, the different sets will not get mixed up.

- Divide the class into groups of four.
  Students read Situation 1. Explain that they are in a maze − see the illustration. They must work together until they get out of the maze. For each situation there is a choice of decisions, and they must talk together until they agree on the correct decision to make. Tell students to read the choice of decisions, **a**, **b**, or **c**, and start discussing.

- What generally happens is that students take a while to make their first decision, but then speed up a little as they grasp the nature of the activity and realize that the situation cards keep coming!

- Monitor the groups, but there should be no need for you to intervene in any way. It is entirely up to the students to 'work their way out of the maze'.

- You should have a set of the situation cards for each group of four students. Keep them separate, and away from the students! As a group makes a decision, they should tell you what situation card they want next. You give it to them, and they continue to negotiate.

- This continues until the group gets to Situation 20, 21, or 22, which have the words 'You have come to the end of the maze'. Of these, only number 20 represents a successful completion of the activity. The other two end in bad health or bankruptcy.

- The group is then invited to do the post-maze activity in the Student's Book. This serves two purposes. It provides further free speaking practice as students are very keen to evaluate their performance and see where they went wrong; and it gives the groups which finish first something to do.

2

You do some market research into the wallpaper business. There are a lot of traditional, well-established firms who have most of the market, but you think that there is a gap for high-class, high-quality expensive wallpaper and matching curtains. Maybe you do have some artistic ability after all!

You design some patterns and approach a manufacturer. He could produce the wallpaper for a few thousand pounds. You also need some money to get an office and do some advertising. Basically, you need money! Where are you going to go to get it?

a The bank. Your credit is good but you'd have to pay interest. **GO TO 5.**

b Your father. He could lend you the money, but you fell out a few years ago and haven't spoken since. Still, he wouldn't want to see you and your family on the street. **GO TO 14.**

c Sell your car. It's in good condition and you'd get the money quickly. You could be selling wallpaper by the end of the month. **GO TO 12.**

3

Success! You go for interviews, and are offered two jobs. Which one are you going to accept?

a One is well-paid, but boring. It wouldn't be much of a challenge, but you need the money. **GO TO 13.**

b One looks quite interesting, but it isn't very well-paid. However, the risk might be worth it. **GO TO 9.**

4

Working as a sales representative pays the bills, but you don't enjoy it very much. You're better at it than you thought. One evening, you're lying in the bath when you have an idea — start your own business! But what? You look up for inspiration. A wallpaper business! Then you realize that you have no money and no artistic ability.

What are you going to do?

a Carry on being a sales representative. It's relatively secure, and after all the months of no income, it's nice to have a regular pay cheque. **GO TO 13.**

b Spend your last money on some market research to see if your idea for a wallpaper business might work. It's a gamble that could leave you homeless. **GO TO 2.**

5

You go to the bank to get some capital. The bank manager is impressed with the market research you have done, and thinks your idea could work. He is prepared to lend you some money, but not all that you need. The bank will provide only half.

Where are you going to get the other half?

a Mortgage your house. This would easily provide enough money, but if the business failed, you'd lose the roof over your head. **GO TO 16.**

b Try your father. He might be more interested now that the bank has said they're willing to lend you 50 per cent. **GO TO 7.**

6

You go on a luxurious holiday abroad. You have a lovely time. While lying on the beach, you have an idea for a small business — start a wallpaper firm! Then you realize you have no money and no artistic ability.

You get back home. What are you going to do?

a Start applying for jobs. You've seen several jobs that you are qualified to do. **GO TO 3.**

b Spend your last money on some market research to see if your idea for a wallpaper business might succeed. It's a gamble that might leave you homeless. **GO TO 2.**

7

You go to your father to borrow the rest of the money you need. Surprise, surprise! He's interested, and is prepared to lend you the money, but on one condition. He wants a share in the business. What are you going to do?

a Accept. He might not interfere too much, and you've still got your house. **GO TO 16.**

b Refuse. You couldn't possibly work with him. **GO TO 11.**

8

The job doesn't turn out to be as interesting as you thought it would be, and the pay is terrible. You decide to leave. You still have some savings.

What are you going to do?

a Go on the retraining scheme — it might lead to a new career. **GO TO 10.**

b Have a holiday. You feel even more depressed. **GO TO 6.**

9

You have an interesting job. It's enjoyable, and you're doing well. After a while, there is a chance of promotion, but the new job would mean you have to spend six months of the year away from your family.

Do you accept the promotion?

a Yes. **GO TO 13.**

b No. **GO TO 8.**

10

You go on a retraining scheme to become a sales representative. It's a six-month course and your savings have nearly all gone. Working in selling doesn't appeal to you very much. You're not very good at it because you're not aggressive enough, and you don't like having to tell lies to sell things to people that they don't really want. What are you going to do?

a Apply for jobs in the textile industry. You've seen several jobs that you're qualified to do. **GO TO 3.**

b Have a holiday. You feel a break would do you good. **GO TO 6.**

c Apply for jobs as a sales representative. After all, you've done the course. **GO TO 4.**

11

If you want to carry on with the idea of the small business, you have no choice. You have to mortgage your house. **GO TO 16.**

12

You have decided to sell your car. You get a good price, but then you realize that you can't go round all the wallpaper shops without transport. What a mistake! **GO BACK TO 2.**

13

You do well in your new job, but unfortunately technology replaces you again. You're made redundant.
GO BACK TO 1.

14

You go to your father. He thinks you're irresponsible and isn't prepared to help. He wants you to 'stand on your own two feet', which is what he had to do.
GO BACK TO 2.

15

Your strategy didn't work. Your business goes bankrupt. This is the end of the maze.

You can either stop and do the post-maze activity on page 25 of the Student's Book, or go back to **16** and try again.

16

You now have the capital you need. The manufacturer makes your wallpaper, and it looks very good. People seem interested in it, and want to see your price list. You have to decide how much you're going to sell your wallpaper for.

What are you going to do?

a Price your wallpaper quite low. This will get the market interested in your product. You can raise your prices later. **GO TO 15.**

b Price it so that you break even — you don't make any profit, but you don't lose any more money. **GO TO 17.**

c Charge high prices. After all, this is a quality product, and if it's cheap the public will think it's inferior. **GO TO 22.**

17

Success! Your business begins to do very well. The public like your wallpaper and you are featured in *Home and Garden Magazine*. After five years your business is well-established then disaster strikes.

If you mortgaged your house, **GO TO 18.**

If you borrowed money from your father, **GO TO 19.**

18

The housing market is in chaos, and the loan that you got with your house as security must be repaid.

What are you going to do?

a Fight on. You're determined to become a millionaire, and this little problem isn't going to stop you. **GO TO 21.**

b Sell your business to pay the debt. Someone offered to buy it at quite a good price a few weeks ago. Anyway, you've had enough of wallpaper. **GO TO 20.**

19

Your father is as kind to his family as J.R. is in Dallas. He wants to buy you out of the business so that all the profit is his.

What are you going to do?

a Fight him. You haven't worked for all these years to give up an extremely profitable business. **GO TO 21.**

b Sell him your part of the business. He offers you a reasonable price, and anyway, you've had enough of wallpaper. **GO TO 20.**

20

You sell your business and get a good price.

You decide to move to the south coast and you live off the interest of your money. You lead a life of comfort and happiness.

You have come to the end of the maze.

Do the post-maze activity on page 25 of the Student's Book.

21

You fight on, work even harder and make even more money.

The pressure of working a sixteen-hour day gives you a heart attack.

You have to give up work.

You have come to the end of the maze.

Do the post-maze activity on page 25 of the Student's Book.

22

Your strategy didn't work. Your business goes bankrupt. This is the end of the maze.

You can either stop and do the post-maze activity on page **25** of the Student's Book, or go back to **16** and try again.

● Listening

Aims

- fluency
- to develop students' listening abilities.

- Introduction: Students in groups of four discuss their first job.
  What was it?
  Where was it?
  What did you have to do?
  How much were you paid?
  Did you enjoy it?

- Play the tape. Students discuss their answers to the pre-set questions, then listen to the tape again to check. This could be done as students read the tapescript.

  Answers

  1 She wanted to 'settle herself and her husband into their new home', that is, to set up and establish a new home, before getting a job.
  2 No, she didn't, because on the first day she was asked to teach at the local junior school.
  3 A local school, with many different nationalities, small, on a hill outside Tanga.
  4 There was snake drill, but instead of running away, the children would run to the snake. Either they or the caretaker would chop the snake's head off.
  5 She didn't want to slap the children as she had been told to do, and she never had discipline problems.
  6 Because it was all she knew about geography.

- Students work in pairs to correct the summary.

Answers

Liz hoped that she too would be able to teach. (No — she didn't know what kind of job it would be.)

She was asked to teach . . . because of her valuable university experience. (No — it was because she was a graduate, and the school was going to close down.)

She found the job difficult . . . because the children were unused to discipline. (No — she found the job difficult, but it was not because the children were unused to discipline.)

She didn't know enough about the subjects she was teaching. (This is partly true, but she had a good knowledge of Swedish geography.)

Language focus
Aims

- accuracy
- to provide students with controlled practice of gerunds in certain expressions with **go**, and practice of gerunds and infinitives generally.

- Do the Controlled Practice exercises 5 and 6 in pairs or small groups.

Answers

5 a. *went shopping*
  b. *am going fishing*
  c. *go skiing/go tobogganing*
  d. *go sailing*
  e. *went swimming*
6 a. *to find*
  b. *looking after*
  c. *to pay*
  d. *overdrawing*
  e. *redecorating*
  f. *to buy*
  g. *to save*
  h. *earning*
  i. *to visit*
  j. *going*
  k. *working*
  l. *to stay*
  m. *being able*
  n. *leaving*
  o. *to miss*

● Writing
Aims

- accuracy
- to develop students' awareness of the style and conventions of a formal letter.

- Introduction: Ask students what they already know about the organization of a formal letter.

Where does your address go?
Where does the address of the person you're writing to go?
How do you begin the letter?
How do you end the letter?
Where do you put your name?
Are there contractions?

- Read the instructions all together. Students correct the letter in pairs.

Sample answer

```
                                18, Kings Road,

                                Birmingham.

                                (date)

Trans Europe Tours,

Bridge Street,

Cambridge.


Dear Mr Bradley,

I saw your advertisement for travel couriers in the

February edition of the magazine Sunshine Holidays.


I have a degree in modern languages, and I speak French,

German, Spanish and a little Greek.  I have travelled

widely in Europe, and I have a particular interest in

French and Italian art.


I think I have several of the qualities necessary to be

a successful guide.


I look forward to hearing from you.  If you would like

to contact me by telephone, my number is 381229.


Yours sincerely,

James Henderson

James Henderson
```

21

- Students correct the envelope.

Answer

Mr Peter Bradley,

Trans Europe Tours,

Bridge Street,

CAMBRIDGE,

CB3 0HR.

REVISION

Aims

- accuracy
- to provide students with controlled and freer practice of short answers, and **so do I/neither do I**, etc.

- Short answers and **so do I/neither do I** present no great conceptual problems, but are quite tricky to manipulate, as students must transfer the correct auxiliary from the statement.
- Students do exercise 1 alone. Only they know the answers. Check what they write.
- Students do exercise 2 in pairs. When the other students correct the sentences, insist on appropriate intonation and contrastive sentence stress.

Example

No, it doesn't.   It rises in the east.

- Students do exercise 3 in pairs. Notice that the auxiliary is not in fact necessary in the replies, but short answers are a feature of the language that English speakers like to use. So in answer to a, students might say *Peter*, but insist on *Peter was*.

- In the **so do I/neither do I** exercise, students have to stand up and 'mingle' for five or six minutes, asking and answering questions. When they have the right information about several of their colleagues, students sit down and write some sentences.
  Ask one or two students to read out their sentences. Again, insist on appropriate intonation and sentence stress.

UNIT 4

Question forms

Is there anybody there?

AIMS OF THE UNIT

- Students at this level of English should be reading as much as possible about whatever interests them. This unit includes the theme of reading literature and light classics, and suggests ways of approaching longer texts. Students read an extract from a popular novel, and are given guidance in writing an appraisal of a book or film.

- The vocabulary exercises revise guessing meaning, which was introduced in Unit 2, examine the dramatic style of an author, and explore the sound/spelling relationship in English. There is an exercise where students must work out the spelling of words that they have only heard, not seen.

- The language input of this unit concentrates on question formation: even at upper-intermediate level, students still require plenty of practice in forming questions correctly.

NOTES ON THE LANGUAGE INPUT

Question formation

Question formation does not present students with great conceptual problems, but they make many mistakes of form.

This unit deals with the following:
question words
how + adjective or adverb
what/which + noun
questions with a preposition at the end
subject/object questions
indirect questions
tag questions

Common mistakes

When you go home?
What you do tonight?
To who did you talk?
About what did you talk?
Who did break the window?
I don't know what are you talking about?
It's raining, doesn't it?

NOTES ON THE UNIT
● **Discussion point**
Aims

- fluency
- free speaking to launch the theme of superstition and the supernatural.

- Discuss the first question all together. All the superstitions either bring good or bad luck, or are to ward off bad luck. In the opinion of the authors, none of them can be explained logically, with the possible exception of *Keep your fingers crossed*, which is related to the symbol of the cross in the Christian religion.

- Encourage the discussion at this point, and especially try to elicit the superstitions from your students'

countries. This can be a fascinating subject.

- Read the dictionary entry all together. The aim is to make the point that one person's belief is another person's superstition. A certain amount of sensitivity is needed here, as devout members of the class could rightly resent their faith being referred to as a superstition.

- Students answer question 3 in groups. This should produce an entertaining and fruitful discussion, and students should be encouraged to add their own personal superstitions.

● **Reading and question formation**
Aims

- the aim of the question formation exercises is accuracy
- the aim of the reading is fluency
- to show students how to approach a book by exploiting their prior knowledge and ability to predict.

- Efficient reading will depend, among other factors, on students transferring the skills they possess in their own language to English. When we pick up a book, we use the cover, the illustrations, the publisher, the author, the title, the 'blurb', and the reviews to make all sorts of guesses about its content. We decide what *kind* of story it is, whether it is fact or fiction, and we build up a picture of what the story will be about.

The aim of questions 1 and 2 is to show students that it is possible to do all this in English. This should be stressed to help students in their own reading in English. See page v of the Teacher's Book.

- Students work in pairs to write in the questions.

Answers

a. *When was it written?*
b. *What sort of book is it?*
c. *Is it fact or fiction?*
d. *What's it about?*
e. *Has it been made into a film?*
f. *Who are the main characters?*
g. *What happens in the story?*
h. *How does it end? What happens in the end?*
i. *What did you think of it?*
j. *Would you recommend it?*

- Question 2 must be done very thoroughly. Most of the questions can be answered, and students must be encouraged to *guess* the answers to the rest.

Example

What's it about?
It's obviously about a little girl who has nightmares. The book is compared to The Exorcist, *so it must be quite a horrific story about the terrible things that happen to her and her family. Perhaps she does awful things like trying to kill her father; perhaps her father thinks a spirit has taken her over that needs to be exorcized. It's sure to be quite a violent story, and probably quite a sad one.*

- Encourage students to formulate other questions that they would like answered.

Examples

Is it based on a true story?
Why does Elliot Hoover think Ivy is his daughter?

- Answer the eight questions based on the front and back cover of *Audrey Rose*. These are to ensure that students have a grasp of the characters and the background before reading the extracts.

Answers

Ivy is a pretty, happy, nine year-old girl who lives in New York.
Her parents are Bill and Janice Templeton.
Elliot Hoover's daughter was killed in a burning car.
Nine years ago.
Presumably, her name was Audrey Rose.
Elliot Hoover believes his daughter's soul entered the body of Ivy.
Presumably it is Ivy that has nightmares.
Perhaps about being in a fire.

- Read the introduction to the extract all together, and ask some check questions.

Example

What does Hoover want?
Why?
How do Ivy's parents feel?
Why?

- Students read the first extract, and answer the Comprehension Check questions 1–3 in pairs or small groups.

Encourage students to use the next extract to formulate questions about what they want to learn.

Continue in this way till the end.

Answers

1 *She is moving about.*
2 *About being in a fire.*
3 *She had the same nightmares.*
4 *No, she doesn't.*
5 *Because she is trying to escape from something.*
6 *It seems as though she is trying to get out of the room via the door or the window.*
7 *Because she imagines that the glass is hot, and so she cannot touch it.*
8 *A man who helped them last time Ivy had nightmares.*
9 *Terribly sad.*
10 *Because he believes that the girl who is having the nightmare is his daughter, Audrey, as she was dying in the car.*
11 *Because he didn't want to believe that his daughter was possessed by the soul of Hoover's daughter.*
12 *Extremely disturbed and anxious.*
13 *She seems to recognize the voice, and calms down. Her fear disappears and the nightmare ends.*
14 *She is afraid, because Ivy's reaction to Hoover seemed to suggest that she recognized him, and she called him Daddy.*

- Answer the 'What do you think?' questions all together.

Answer

1 *The moment in the book is significant because it seems to prove that what Hoover says is true, and that Ivy is possessed by the soul of his dead daughter. Ivy's parents will now have to recognize this, even though they don't want to believe it.*

There are no prescribed answers to questions 2 and 3.

Language focus

Aims

- accuracy
- to provide students with controlled practice in forming **wh-** questions, questions with **like** used as a verb and a preposition, subject and object questions, and questions with prepositions.

- Read the Language Review all together.

- Sentences for translation (see page iv of the Teacher's Book).

How big is your house?
What films have you seen recently?
Which soup would you like?
Who did you dance with?
Who did you give it to?
What did Peter break?
Who broke the window?

- Students can read the Grammar section in class or at home. It is not very long.

- Do the Controlled Practice exercises 1–4.

Answers

The answers for question 1 are mainly sample answers, as students have a certain choice in how they complete the questions.

1.
  a. *How often do you go to the cinema?*
  b. *What colour are your eyes?*
  c. *How far is it from here to your house?*
  d. *Whose is this jumper?*
  e. *What size trousers do you take?*
  f. *Which airline did you fly?/What's your favourite airline?*
  g. *How many times have you been to Russia?*
  h. *Who did you talk to?*
  i. *How much do you spend on petrol?*
  j. *Which channel is the film on?*
  k. *What was the weather like?*
  l. *How long does it take you to get to work?*
  m. *What have you done to your hair?*
  n. *Which newspaper do you read?*
  o. *What sort of stories do you like?*

2.
  a. *What's he like?*
  b. *What does she look like?*
  c. *What does he like doing?*
  d. *Would you like to go out tonight?*
  e. *What was the film like?/Did you like the film?*

3. Many questions are possible here. You need to check students' answers very carefully, to make sure they have seen the difference between a subject and an object question.

4.
  a. *Where to?*   e. *What for?*
  b. *What about?*   f. *What about?*
  c. *Who from?*   g. *Who to?*
  d. *Who with?*   h. *What with?*

● Vocabulary 1

Aims

- accuracy
- to revise the technique of guessing the meaning of unknown vocabulary by exploiting linguistic and contextual clues
- to highlight the dramatic style of *Audrey Rose.*

– Students work in pairs to try to guess the meaning of the words from *Audrey Rose.* Remind students that understanding everything is often not necessary, and that they should try to work out what part of speech the unfamiliar item is. You should also remind them to examine the context and to make use of their knowledge of prefixes and suffixes. This latter point will help with many of the items.

Example

tightly
helplessly
ineffective
inexpressible
breathless

– Read the introduction to exercise 2 all together, then students do it in pairs. This is a very interesting exercise that students generally enjoy very much. Although many of the words in column A may be new to them, by examining the context of *Audrey Rose* and looking at the words in column B, they can do it quite easily.

Answers

A	B
terrified	*frightened*
oblivious of	*unaware of*
feverish	*hot*
plunge	*dive*
grasped	*held*
macabre	*horrible*
tormented	*troubled*
observing	*looking at*
seeking	*looking for*
to seize	*to take hold of*
rapid	*fast*
rose	*got louder*
brilliant	*bright*
clutching	*holding*

● Listening

Aims

- fluency
- to practise students' listening abilities
- to practise taking notes whilst listening.

– Do the Pre-listening task all together. This is a sort of chain

story, where each student must add a few lines for the next student to pick up on and continue. Depending on the number of students in your class, this could go round several times, for as long as they are all still interested.

– Before you play the tape, ask students to look at the headings under which they must take notes, and in pairs *guess* what they might hear.

– As students listen to the tape, they take notes. This exercise is for gist listening rather than intensive listening, and students are not expected to make lengthy notes.

– After hearing the tape for the first time, students work in pairs to compare notes. Then they listen again, perhaps whilst reading the tapescript at the same time.

– Answer the 'What do you think?' questions all together. This should develop into a useful discussion, as the supernatural is a subject that has wide appeal. Encourage students to talk about stories they have heard and experiences they have had.

Language focus
Aims

- accuracy
- to provide students with controlled practice of indirect questions, and practice in recognizing and producing correct intonation in tag questions.

– Do the Controlled Practice exercises 5–9.
Remind students that in indirect questions there is no **do/does/did.**

Answers

5 Students can begin with any of the suggestions.
  a. *I wonder/I'd like to know* etc. *what the ghost's name was.*
  b. . . . *if it is still there.*
  c. . . . *whether it ever came back.*
  d. . . . *why Stephanie thought she was being watched.*

e. *. . . if she saw a ghost when she was young.*

f. *. . . how long the ghost had been haunting the house.*

g. *. . . why it was so cold when the ghost came.*

h. *. . . if Stephanie was telling the truth.*

- Students work in pairs to do exercises 6 and 7. Emphasize that these are accuracy-based activities, and great care must be taken to form questions correctly. You could record some of the pairs, and play back the interview for intensive correction.

- Students have great problems in producing tag questions accurately for several reasons. In many languages there is a set phrase (e.g. *n'est-ce pas?; nicht wahr?*) where English has many variables. However, the greatest problem is intonation. Students find it very difficult to produce the type (i) question tag where the voice falls, because in many languages questions always rise. In general, only the more able students attempt to produce tag questions, although most students can respond to them appropriately. Read the introduction to exercise 8 all together, and drill the two sentences.

Before playing the tape, you could say a few tag questions yourself, and ask students to say if they are type (i) or type (ii).

Example

It's a nice day today, isn't it? (i)
You haven't seen my pen anywhere, have you? (ii)
Play the tape. Students write which type the eight tag questions are.

Answers

a. (i)	d. (ii)	g. (ii)
b. (ii)	e. (i)	h. (i)
c. (ii)	f. (i)	

- Students write some tag questions to ask another member of the class. Be vigilant in your correction of intonation, checking which type of tag question students are trying to produce.

● Vocabulary 2
Aims

- accuracy
- to explore the sound/spelling relationship in English, particularly vowel sounds
- to practise finding a word in the dictionary when the spelling must be guessed.

- English spelling is notoriously non-phonetic, and this situation is made worse by the fact that English has twenty vowel sounds (including diphthongs) where Spanish and Italian, for example, have far fewer. The poem should be treated with a certain light-heartedness, otherwise students might well throw up their hands in dismay! There is a frustrating lack of logic in the pronunciation of, for example, **hose**, **dose** and **lose**.

- Read the introduction, and establish the two ways in which students can work out the pronunciation of the words in italics.

- Students work in groups of three to practise the poem. As they are reading, go round the groups monitoring and correcting.

- After a while, ask one student (preferably one who you expect to do quite well) to read the poem out loud while the rest of the class listens. Correct any mistakes intensively, drilling the words around all the class as appropriate. Then ask students to practise it again in pairs or small groups.

- Students do exercise 2 in pairs.

Answers

a. *break, pay, say, paid*

b. *weak*

c. *sew, low, foe, hose, dose, comb, roll, home, mould, lone*

d. *few, shoe, lose, goose, choose, tomb, food*

e. *horse, cord*

f. *worse, heard, word*

g. *beard*

h. *cow*

i. *bomb, doll, gone*

j. *some, blood, done*

k. *said*

l. *good, could*

- Do exercise 3 all together.

Sample answers

a. *ache, cake, taste*

b. *thief, people, Peter, police*

c. *boat, though*

d. *June, soup, fruit, true*

e. *saw, walk, war, daughter*

f. *burn, shirt, journey*

g. *beer*

h. *found*

i. *wash, cough*

j. *run, enough, does*

k. *end, head, says, Leicester*

l. *push*

- Students work in pairs to do exercise 4.

Play the tape through, asking some check questions, then play it again and stop the recorder after the pauses. Students talk together to discuss the possible spelling, then try to find it in the dictionary. When about half the class have found it (some pairs will take a long time to find the right spelling and the right definition), ask one of the students who knows the spelling to tell the others.

This is an extremely useful skill to practise, and one which students usually find beneficial and satisfying. It can easily be done with any tape you might use.

● Speaking
Aims

- fluency
- to provide students with an opportunity for free speaking.

- This activity is launched by means of the previous listening exercise. Students fill in the boxes for themselves.

- When they have done this, conduct the class survey all together. Ask questions such as the following:

Did any of you put 10 in the boxes? Which ones?
What was your highest score?
How many people had (e.g. Spiders) as their highest score?

- Answer the remaining questions all together.

● Writing

Aims

- accuracy
- to give students guidance in writing an appraisal of a book or film.

- Introduction: Ask students about their favourite book/film, or a book/film they have read/seen recently.

  What was it about?
  Why did they like it?

- Students work in groups of three to compare the organization of the two appraisals.

  The first has no logical order; personal impressions are mixed up with factual information about the story; it repeats itself; the names of the characters are not introduced; we aren't told what sort of story it is; above all, we do not learn *why* the writer liked the book.

  The second gives important factual information at the start, plus an overall impression of the book. The characters are carefully introduced and their background explained. Sufficient information about the plot is given, so the reader has an idea of what happens and why. The title is explained. The appraisal ends with further personal impressions.

- Students do questions 2–5 in small groups.

Answers

2 There are no set divisions. One possibility is the following:
Paragraph 1 ends after *as it progresses*.
Paragraph 2 ends after *by her every move*.
Paragraph 3 ends after *most precious 'butterfly'*.
Paragraph 4 ends after *nothing to help*.

Purpose of each paragraph:

Paragraph 1 Background factual information – when, what, who by
Initial personal opinion.
Paragraph 2 Background to story and main characters, especially him.

Paragraph 3 The basic plot.
Paragraph 4 An aspect of the story that interested the writer. The ending.
Paragraph 5 Conclusion. Final personal impression.

3 Present Simple, because the story is not a past event – it is 'always true'.

4 *first published in*
horror story
one of the most . . . I have ever . . .
It holds your attention . . .
. . . as it progresses
title
hero
his background
understand his behaviour
We see him . . .
a turning point
One of the most interesting aspects of the . . . is the portrayal of . . .
In the end . . .
the final . . . outcome
impossible to put down

5 Because he is not really a hero and she is not a real butterfly.

- Students write their own appraisal for homework. Tell them to read the instructions and the suggestions carefully.

REVISION

Aims

- accuracy
- to sort out the confusion caused for students by the verb **have**.

- For obvious reasons, students have difficulty manipulating the verb **have**.

  Read the introduction all together, and then the Grammar reference.

- Students do exercises 1 and 2 in pairs or small groups. The questions follow the order of the uses presented in the introduction.

Answers

1 a. *She hasn't been to America.*
  b. *I don't have a bath every night.*

  c. *She hasn't got long hair.*
  d. *They don't have to work very hard.*

2 a. *How many books has he written?*
  b. *When do you have lunch?*
  c. *What sort of car has he got?*
  d. *What time do you have to get up?*

- Students do exercises 3 and 4 in pairs or small groups.

Answers

3 a. *I had a holiday in Mexico last year.*
  b. *I had my first car when I was 19.*
  c. *I had to work hard when I was at school.*

4 a. *We're having a good time at the party.*
  b. *She hasn't got much experience of working with children.*
  c. *We've got a lovely room with a view over the ocean.*
  d. *The restaurant hasn't got any red wine, so we've got to have white.*
  e. *He's having a row with his neighbour.*

- There is no freer practice of **have** because it will come up all the time in the course of your lessons. Note not only the occasions when it is used wrongly, but also when it is used correctly.

There is a progress text on the first four units of *Headway Upper-Intermediate* in the Workbook.

UNIT 5

Narrative tenses

Travel and transport

AIMS OF THE UNIT

- The language input of the unit concentrates on narrative tenses; that is, Past Simple, Past Continuous, Past Perfect Simple and Past Perfect Continuous.

- The Writing section deals with conjunctions and prepositions of time, which are important in narrating past events.

- In the vocabulary work, students are introduced to homonyms and homophones, which are extremely common in English, and shown how they are used in jokes to make puns.

NOTES ON THE LANGUAGE INPUT

Narrative tenses

Students at this level will of course have a certain familiarity with the Past Simple and Past Continuous, and generally use them quite appropriately. The aspect of the Past Continuous which is most often presented to students, and which is easiest to understand, is to describe an activity interrupted by an event which is expressed in the Past Simple. However, there is a more subtle use of the Past Continuous: it can be used as a 'backdrop', to describe and introduce the events of the narrative which happen 'centre stage'.

Example

I studied languages at university.
The simple tense focuses on the completed action as a whole.

James cursed as he drove along the motorway.
The simple is used, not the continuous, even though the actions were repeated.

The rain was pouring down, and lorries were overtaking on the inside lane.
The writer does not see these two activities as centre stage, but as background.

It rained every day of our holidays.
The writer is interested in the plain, 'simple' fact.

This aspect is explored in the Language Review, the Controlled Practice and the Workbook.

Students are introduced to the Past Perfect Simple and Continuous. The aspect of 'an action before another action in the past' is not difficult to explain or understand, and exists in many other languages. Again, students need to perceive the elements of meaning conveyed by the Continuous tense. The relationship between the Past Perfect Simple and Continuous is the same as between the Present Perfect Simple and Continuous, that is, completed action as opposed to repeated activity.

Example

A *What have you been doing? You're covered in paint!*
B *I've just finished painting the bathroom.*

John seemed surprised when he saw me. I was covered in paint because I
had been decorating, and I hadn't noticed that my hair was in fact yellow.

NOTES ON THE UNIT
 Vocabulary 1

Aims

- the aim of the vocabulary input is accuracy
- the aim of the discussion is fluency, and to launch the theme of travel.

- Introduction: Ask students what their favourite form of transport is, and why. Encourage discussion and questions.

- Students work in pairs to divide the means of transport into three groups, using dictionaries if necessary.

- The success of exercise 2 depends to a certain extent on students' imagination. If they can begin to 'let it flow', an interesting discussion will ensue as they exchange their associations and images connected with some of the forms of transport. Gently probe with your questions.

Example

If a student says he/she finds trams romantic, ask questions such as the following:

Why do you think that?
Where have you seen trams? In photographs or films?
Have you ever been on a tram?
What period in history do you associate trams with?

- Students can do question 3 in groups or all together. The topic is of universal interest, and the discussion could last a long time if you so wish.

● Reading
Aims
- fluency
- to develop students' reading abilities
- to practise marking a text for summary.

- Students do the two Pre-reading tasks in groups. Be prepared to feed in vocabulary as students are answering the question about what can go wrong on the ground and in the air, for example: **hijack; hit an air pocket; delays; overbooking; luggage misdirected**.

- Students read the article quickly to find the answer to the two questions, *Was their order of importance the same?* and *Did they mention any of the problems you discussed?* Set a time limit of thirty seconds for this — encouraging speed reading is very important. Then let students read in more detail.

- Students do the Comprehension Check questions in pairs or small groups.

Answers

1 Students might argue that all except the collision with airport trucks could have happened both on the ground and in the air, but this is 'stretching the point' a little. Hijacks, engine failure, trouble with landing gear, lightning strikes, food poisoning, and near misses occur more often in the air; bomb scares can occur both in the air and on the ground.

2 – *double booking of 747*
   – *overbooking three times on African airline*
   – *man in shirt and trousers stuck outside plane*
   – *pilot stuck outside plane*
   – *passenger asked to sit in lavatory*
   – *lifeboat drill on flight between London and Manchester*
   – *pieces of engine fall off*
   – *passenger asked to hold door shut*
   – *baggage misdirected*

3 *Because the local military decided that that was the way to see who should get on the plane.*

4 *Because they had been locked out.*

5 *Because the plane doesn't go over water.*

6 *Films.*
  No.

7 *Because his luggage had been misdirected.*

- Answer the 'What do you think?' questions all together.

- Students work in pairs to compose a dialogue. The aim is semi-controlled practice of narrative tenses.

- Students work alone to mark the text to summarize it. Stress that they should mark the minimum. When they have done it, they compare their summaries in pairs.

Language focus
Aims
- accuracy
- to compare and contrast Past Simple and Continuous and to provide controlled practice
- to practise the pronunciation of **-ed** in regular past tenses and past participles
- to practise students' ability to recognize weak forms.

- Read the Language Review all together.

- Sentences for translation (see page iv of the Teacher's Book).

  When we arrived, she made some coffee.
  When we arrived, she was making some coffee.
  What were you doing at 6.00 last night?
  I read a book last night.
  I was reading War and Peace.

- Students read the Grammar section for homework.

- Do the Controlled Practice exercises 1–5.
  Students do exercise 1 in pairs.

Answers

a. In the first sentence, two Past Simple tenses show that one action followed another.
   In the second sentence, the Past Continuous shows that the announcement began *before* I arrived.

b. The first sentence suggests I finished the book; the second suggests I didn't.

c. The first sentence in the Past Simple focuses on the completed action as a whole.
   The second sentence with the Past Continuous shows the activity was interrupted.

d. The first sentence contains two Past Simple tenses, which show that one action followed another. In the second sentence, it was snowing before we arrived.

- Do exercise 2 all together. The main tense used will be the Past Simple.

- Do exercise 3 all together. The main tense used will be the Past Continuous.

- Students do exercise 4 in pairs.

Answers

/t/ *searched panicked laughed mixed reached developed*

/d/ *robbed scared banged climbed managed staggered*

/ɪd/ *needed shouted wounded added persuaded hunted*

- Students do the dictation on their own, then check their answers with the tapescript.
  The aim is for students to recognize weak forms when they are pronounced at natural speed. Not only auxiliary verbs, but also function words such as **at, as, for, but**, and **to**, have their vowel sounds reduced, mainly to the 'schwa' sound /ə/.

- See the Workbook for further contrastive work on the Past Simple and Past Continuous.

● Vocabulary 2

Aims
- accuracy
- to introduce students to homonyms and homophones.

- English is particularly rich in words that have multiple meanings (homonyms), and because English spelling is not phonetic, many words that are spelt differently are in fact pronounced the same (homophones). Both cause problems when students are listening, and homonyms cause problems when they are reading.

  Read 1 all together.

- Students work in pairs to do question 2.

  Answers

a. *leave*	e. *fine*
b. *sound*	f. *fair*
c. *will*	g. *swallow*
d. *draw*	h. *saw*

- Students work in pairs to do question 3.

  Answers

  male - mail
  caught - court
  wear - where
  stair - stare
  die - dye

  war - wore
  piece - peace
  hole - whole
  rain - reign
  bored - board

  hire - higher
  through - threw
  way - weigh
  saw - sore
  pair - pear

- Students read the jokes at their own speed. A smile or a laugh will prove comprehension, but don't be disappointed if this doesn't happen! It is difficult to appreciate humour in a different language, especially when it is verbal humour. Remember, too, that these are children's jokes and may not have the same appeal for adults!

● Speaking

Aims
- fluency
- to provide students with an opportunity for free speaking.

- Students work in pairs or small groups to add as many points as they can to each section. It is usually quite easy to think of good and bad points, but it requires some objective, 'lateral' thinking to add interest points which are neither good nor bad.

- When the groups have sufficient ideas, compare them all together. What is interesting is that often good and bad points cancel each other out, or contradict each other. For example, a good point is that we can see how people in different cultures live but, as it says in the example, a bad point is that countries are losing their individuality, so cultures and customs are disappearing. It might be valuable to explore this with the points your students make.

- Students discuss the questions in 2 all together or in small groups.

● Listening

Aims
- fluency
- to develop students' listening abilities
- to practise prediction and anticipation.

- Introduction: Ask students if they have ever driven a large vehicle. What is difficult about driving a bus or a lorry?

- Read the introduction together and play the first part of the tape. Stop the tape after 'Don't worry, you'll be all right!'

- Answer the five questions all together. This is just to establish the background to the story.

- Students work in small groups, looking at the words and imagining the story. It isn't necessary for them to write it.
  Ask one or two students to retell the story they imagined.

- Play the rest of the tape. Students put numbers 1 to 5 on the map, and write one or two notes describing each incident.

Students compare their maps in pairs.

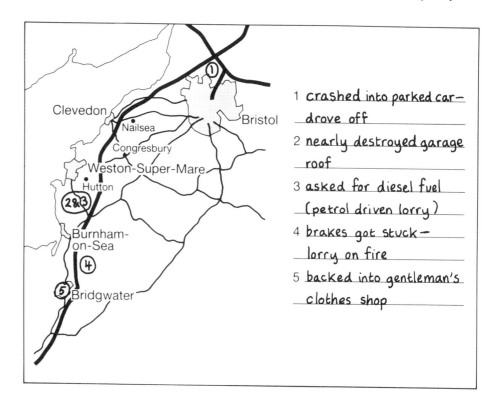

1 crashed into parked car - drove off

2 nearly destroyed garage roof

3 asked for diesel fuel (petrol driven lorry)

4 brakes got stuck - lorry on fire

5 backed into gentleman's clothes shop

- Students work in pairs to answer the Comprehension Check questions.

Answers

1 *When did the story take place?*
2 *What time did he have to go to the fruit market?*
3 *Did he stop when he crashed into the side of a car?*
4 *Why did the man at the petrol station shout at Brian?*
5 *What time did he get to Bridgwater?*
6 *Who said 'Can I help you, sir?'?*

Language focus
Aims

- accuracy
- to compare and contrast Past Perfect and Past Simple; to compare and contrast Past Perfect Simple and Past Perfect Simple and Continuous
- to provide freer practice of narrative tenses, question and answer.

- Students find the examples of the Past Perfect in the tapescript.
- Sentences for translation (see page iv of the Teacher's Book).

  When I arrived at the theatre, the play began.
  When I arrived at the theatre, the play had begun.
  She was happy because she had won a competition.
  I was tired because I had been working for ten hours.

- Do the Controlled Practice exercises 6–8. Students do exercises 6 and 7 in pairs or small groups.

Answers

6 a. *He had been driving for a few seconds.*
  b. *He had crashed into the side of a parked car.*
  c. *Because the brakes had stuck.*
  d. *Because he had been driving for four hours.*
  e. *Because Brian had driven his lorry through the shop window.*

7 a. In the first sentence, the play started after our arrival; in the second, before.

b. In the first sentence, she laughed as soon as she saw the photograph. In the second, she went home some time after all the photographs had been seen.
c. In the first sentence, the Continuous emphasizes the activity. In the second sentence, the Simple emphasizes the completed action.
d. In the first sentence, the Simple is used because it was a single action. In the second sentence, the Continuous expresses a repeated action.

- Do question 8 all together. The main tense used will be the Past Simple, but you can prompt students to use the Past Continuous and the Past Perfect as well.
- See the Workbook for further controlled practice of the Past Perfect.

● Writing
Aims

- accuracy
- to introduce students to conjunctions and prepositions of time.
- to practise narrative tenses.

- Read part 1 all together.
- Students do question 2 in pairs.

Answers

a. *while*   d. *after*
b. *since*   e. *Whenever*
c. *until*

- Students do question 3 on their own.
- Students are asked to work in groups of three to write the story of the businessman. As with any group work, the aim is for students to pool their ideas, and this can be as beneficial with the writing skill as with any other activity. Further advantages are that there should be a greater degree of accuracy, and a more detailed story — students quite naturally tend to tell a story in the shortest possible way, and three heads might have more ideas.

Adequate time should be allowed for this, perhaps twenty minutes. Go round the groups checking and correcting. A spokesperson can read out his/her group's story for the others to comment on.

REVISION
Aims

- accuracy
- to practise common expressions and exclamations.

- Despite the frequency of these expressions, students often confuse them, saying for example, **Excuse me?** when they want something repeated, **Pardon!** when they are trying to get past someone, and not understanding the different meanings of **mind.**
- Students match up the two lines from column A and column B.

Answers

a. *Mind your own business. All right. All right. I didn't mean to be nosy.*
b. *I've changed my mind. What, again?*
c. *Excuse me! Yes, can I help you?*
d. *Mind the step. Ouch! Too late.*
e. *Sorry! Never mind. It doesn't matter.*
f. *Pardon? I'll say it again for you.*
g. *I don't care what he does. That's not very nice. I thought you two were friends.*
h. *It serves him right. Why? What did he do?*
i. *Here you are. Thank you.*
j. *Come on! Where to?*
k. *What's up? I don't feel very well.*
l. *It's up to you. Oh no. I hate decisions.*
m. *Do you want this one or that one? I don't mind. You choose.*

- Students work in pairs to prepare a short dialogue which includes one pair of lines. Allow adequate time for this.
  They read out their dialogues. The rest of the class must guess where

the dialogue is taking place, and
who the people are.

- Do question 2 all together.

Answers

Good luck! Before someone is
taking an exam, for instance.
Congratulations! When someone
has won something, got married, or
had a baby.
Good Lord! When someone is
surprised.
Have a nice time! When someone is
going out.
Cheerio! Colloquial for goodbye.
I'm sorry to hear that. When
someone tells you their bad news.
Bad luck! When they fail.
Watch out! When there is some
danger.
Ta. Slang for 'thank you'.
Cheers! A toast when drinking.

- Question 3 is a fun exercise.
Students work out the meaning from
the context of the tape.

Answers

Hey! To attract attention.
Ouch! To express pain.
Sh! To ask someone to be quiet.
Mmm! To express pleasure.
Boo! To express disapproval,
especially at public meetings.
Oh! To express surprise.
Uh-huh Means 'yes'.
Ugh! To express disgust.
Tut-tut! To express disapproval,
especially to children.
Whoops! When one makes a minor
mistake.

UNIT 6

Expressing quantity

How do you feel today?

AIMS OF THE UNIT

- This unit includes the themes of food, health, and alternative medicine, which are topics that affect us all.
- The language input concentrates on the important area of quantifiers.
- The first vocabulary exercise helps students with the language of statistics, to compare and contrast data, and introduces clauses of comparison.
- The Writing and the Revision sections deal with modal verbs, revising the forms and concepts introduced in *Headway Intermediate*. This serves as preparation for further work on modal verbs in Units 7, 9, 10, and 11.

NOTES ON THE LANGUAGE INPUT

Quantifiers

Quantifiers present students with few conceptual problems, but they make many mistakes of form.

Common mistakes

Some of people have two houses.
There isn't many butter left.
All enjoyed the film except Peter.
He hasn't got some money.
I didn't buy nothing.
It took a long times to get to the airport.

The last mistake is due to a confusion between mass and count nouns. Most nouns are either mass or count, but some can be both.

Example

Mass nouns:
weather, rice, advice, oxygen

Count nouns:
tree, tent, chair, pencil

Mass or count nouns:

wine
Wine is good for you.
The wines of southern France are excellent.

sugar
Sugar is bad for your teeth.
How many sugars do you take?

country
We live in the country.
I've been to most countries in Europe.

This area is dealt with in more depth in Unit 12.

NOTES ON THE UNIT

 Discussion point

Aims

- fluency
- free speaking to launch the theme of food and health
- to test students' abilities in using quantifiers.

- This Discussion Point is one of the longest in the book, and could occupy a good hour if this fits your timetable. If not, leave out question 3.

- Answer question 1 all together. Be prepared to help students with vocabulary problems. This discussion could last a long time, so make sure you leave yourself enough time to answer the other questions in the Discussion Point.

- Answer question 2 all together, sorting out problems of vocabulary as you go, and ensuring that students understand each part. This is preferable to students doing the quiz at their own speed, as it avoids your having to explain the same item again and again! Certain items might be difficult to explain, depending on your students. They might not be aware of the kind of cooking oil they use; they might not know what skimmed milk or Cheddar cheese is; you might have to explain what wholemeal bread is (bread made with the entire wheat kernel, not bleached or purified); a slice of English bread is much larger than, say, a slice of French bread; and jacket potatoes (baked in their skins, sometimes filled with sauces) might be unknown to your students.

- Students add up their scores and read the appropriate interpretation. Encourage discussion at this point by asking for their reactions. Do they agree with the interpretation? How can you cut down on fat?

- To do question 3, students should choose one of the questions from the quiz. If you don't think your students will have particular preferences, allocate a question to them. There are 17 questions. Students stand up and quickly ask everyone in the class, then sit down and prepare their 'report'. The language used in the report, and in the answer to question 4, tests their ability at using the target language of the unit.

- Students work in pairs to think of different kinds of food in question 4. Do the second part of question 4 as a class discussion.

● Reading

Aims

- fluency
- to develop students' reading abilities
- to draw students' attention to spoken versus written style.

- Students work in pairs to check the vocabulary in a dictionary. Make sure they find the correct entry for the words, as there are several potential confusions, for example / li:d / versus / led /, and **liver, grave, vein**, and **stroke** are all homonyms.

Students try to predict some of the health hazards mentioned in the letter. Get the feedback to this, and try to encourage a class discussion. You might have to prompt with questions such as the following:

Why is lead dangerous?
Where do we find it?
What can go wrong with our liver?
What substances are in the atmosphere that might be bad to inhale?

- Students scan the letter to answer the two questions. Set a time limit of two minutes.

Answers

1 No, it wasn't written by a doctor.
2 We cannot know for sure what he is doing at each time, but the answers below are plausible ones.

    7.05 *Standing at the window breathing in the air*
    7.30 *In the bathroom getting ready*
    7.45 *Having breakfast in the kitchen*
    8.30 *Driving to work in his car*
    8.55 *In the lift or climbing the stairs*

    9.00 *Arriving at his office*
    9.10 *In his office, talking to his colleague*
    1.15 *In the pub having lunch*
    4.00 *In his office feeling ill*
    6.00 *Driving home in his car*
    6.30 *Arriving home*

- Students answer the Comprehension Check questions in pairs or small groups.

Answers

1 Breathing the air is dangerous because it is polluted with lead; the lavatory handle is covered with bacteria; tea and coffee are bad for your heart; there is too much fat in an English fried breakfast; nylon toothbrushes are bad for your gums; aerosol sprays are dangerous to inhale; and white bread does not contain sufficient fibre, which is necessary for your digestion.
2 Because it doesn't let your skin breathe, which causes rashes.
3 Just over three kilos. (1 pound = 0.45 kilos; half a stone = 7 pounds).
4 Your family.
5 For the exercise, especially if you are sitting down most of the day.
6 Her make-up might cause cancer.
7 It makes him tense.
8 She has inhaled washing powder (which presumably contains dangerous chemicals), asbestos particles from her hair drier, and the chemicals from aerosol sprays.

- Answer questions 1 and 2 of the 'What do you think?' questions all together.

Answers

1 That knowledge of all the dangers we face has not made us any happier, and has probably made us more mentally unbalanced.
2 Students could argue that either a., b., or c. represents the writer's attitude. In the opinion of the authors, c. is the best answer.

- Students do question 3 on their own and mark the text, then compare with a partner.

- Set up question 4 all together, finding some examples of spoken

English, then asking students to find more examples in pairs or small groups. All the exclamations (*Good Heavens! Horrors!*); rhetorical questions (*Didn't you realize that all that nylon won't let your skin breathe? Eating* must *be good for you – mustn't it?*); asides (*White bread, eh?*), and warnings (*Get out at once and race up those stairs, unless you want a heart attack tomorrow.*) are examples which sound like spoken English.

Language focus

Aims

- accuracy
- to provide students with controlled practice of **some** and **any** and their compounds (**someone**, etc.)
- students listen to short dialogues in various shops and guess what kind of shop it is.

- Read the Language Review all together.

- Sentences for translation (see page iv of the Teacher's Book).
How much cheese have we got?
How many eggs have we got?
We have a little cheese.
I have little money.
We have a few eggs.
I have few close friends.

- Students read the Grammar section for homework, or in class.

- Do the Controlled Practice exercises 1–4.
Students do exercises 1–3 in pairs or small groups.

Answers

  a. *some*   d. *any*
  b. *some*   e. *some, any*
  c. *any*

2 a. *Everyone/everybody*
  b. *everywhere, anywhere*
  c. *nothing*
  d. *nobody/no-one*
  e. *something*
  f. *somewhere*
  g. *anyone/anybody*

3 **Sample answers**
  a. *Everything he cooks is burnt.*
  b. *Someone had broken in and stolen my stereo.*

c. *I've never met anyone as beautiful as you.*
d. *. . . no-one could help me.*
e. *Does anyone want anything?*

- Play the short conversations in exercise 4. Students decide in pairs what sort of shop it is.

Answer
a. *bank*
b. *cheese shop/supermarket/ delicatessen*
c. *butchers*
d. *shoe shop*
e. *bakers*
f. *greengrocers*
g. *hardware shop*
h. *newsagents*

Students will be exploiting contextual and lexical clues to decide wich shop it is. They should be able to guess without knowing all the vocabulary, but you might want to direct them to the tapescript to examine the various vocabulary items (e.g. one-pound coins, Cheddar, lamb chops, rolls, etc.)

● Vocabulary 1

Aims

- accuracy
- to provide help in expressing statistics and comparing and contrasting data.

- Discuss the two quotations all together, and ask students to complete the chart in question 1.

Answers
a slight fall
a gradual fall
a sharp fall

- Students look at the graphs in question 2 and make sentences such as the following:

Life expectancy in Third World countries has risen from 41 in 1950 to 57 in 1985.
In America, it has risen from 71 in 1970 to 74 in 1981.

- Students do question 3 in pairs or small groups.
This requires intensive reading and a good understanding of the graphs, so allow adequate time for students

to do it. You could do the first few together, so students see what they have to do.

Answers
There might occasionally be alternatives to the ones suggested, but make sure that students have interpreted the graphs accurately.
a. *The United States*
b. *a slight fall . . . dropped sharply*
c. *a slight rise . . . numbers have fallen*
d. *United States . . . England and Wales . . . infectious diseases*
e. *cancer . . . heart disease*
f. *strokes or infectious diseases*
g. *Japan*
h. *Japan*
i. *heart disease*
j. *six times*

- Students listen to the tape in question 4 and complete the graph. This requires intensive listening. Play the tape two or three times. Before telling students the correct answer, ask them to read the tapescript and check their graph.

Answer

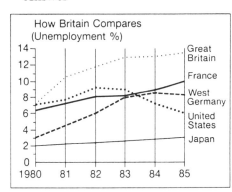

How Britain Compares (Unemployment %)

- Students work in groups to do question 5, to produce sentences such as the following:

In West Germany, there was a gradual increase in the number of unemployed between 1980 and 1983.
There has been a gradual increase in the number of overseas visitors to Britain since 1981.
About a third of the overseas visitors to Britain in 1985 came from North America.
There was a sharp drop in the number of Britons going abroad in 1985.

- There is an exercise in the Workbook that further practises this input.

● Listening

Aims

- fluency
- to develop students' listening abilities
- to practise transferring information from one medium to another.

- Do the Pre-listening task all together. Try to encourage discussion about acupuncture, and other forms of alternative medicine. If you have oriental students in your class, encourage them to give their views on this subject, as the East views medical care very differently from the West.

- Play the tape of the interview with Glenna Gillingham. It is quite long, so ask students to 'sit back and enjoy' it for the first listening, and not worry about completing the chart.

- After the first listening, students talk in pairs and begin to fill in the chart in question 1 of the Comprehension Check questions. Then play the tape again, for students to add more information.

- Students answer the remaining questions in pairs or small groups.

Answers
1 Holistic medicine looks at the body as a whole, western medicine as a series of parts. Western medicine aims to remove the symptoms of an illness, without finding the cause; holistic medicine looks at a person's whole life style to try to find the imbalance. Holistic medicine tries above all to prevent illness.
2 Bob suffered from headaches, but after a few courses he was better. Gill had had arthritis for years, but recovered after six treatments. John had backache for a year and was told to stop drinking coffee.
3 She would like to see Western and holistic medicine working together, in a medical practice where there are four doctors and

an acupuncturist, all working in their own specialist areas.

4 Because people are becoming disillusioned with their own doctor, who has little time to talk to them and merely prescribes pills.

- Do the 'What do you think?' questions all together. This should develop into a productive discussion, and could cover a wide variety of subjects; for example, students' own experiences of both Western and holistic medicine, successful and unsuccessful, 'old wives' tales', etc.

Language focus

Aims

- accuracy
- to provide students with controlled practice of quantifiers.

- Do the Controlled Practice exercises 5–7 in pairs or small groups.

Answers

5 a. *a few*
  b. *a little*
  c. *few*
  d. *little*
  e. *a few*

6 a. *He did a great deal of work.*
     He did a lot of work.
     He did lots of work.
  b. *I've made a great deal of progress.*
     I've made a lot of progress.
     I've made lots of progress.
  c. *They invited a large number of people.*
     They invited a lot of people.
     They invited lots of people.
  d. *There was a great deal of snow last winter.*
     There was a lot of snow last winter.
     There was lots of snow last winter.
  e. *A large number of animals die of starvation in winter.*
     A lot of animals die of starvation in winter.
     Lots of animals die of starvation in winter.

  f. *I read a large number of books, because I have a great deal of free time.*
     I read a lot of books, because I have a lot of free time.
     I read lots of books, because I have lots of free time.

- Students do exercise 7 in pairs. It should be quite light-hearted.

● Vocabulary 2

Aims

- accuracy
- to introduce students to a set of vocabulary to do with illness and health care.

- Students do questions 1 and 2 in pairs or small groups, using dictionaries.

- Students work alone to do question 3. This usually produces some very funny symptoms and diagnoses! Be prepared to help students with vocabulary they may want to know.

● Speaking

Aims

- fluency
- to provide students with an opportunity for free speaking practice.

- Divide students into four groups. They select one of the groups of people they are going to entertain. It doesn't matter if two groups choose the same people, as then the menus can be compared.
  You should expect there to be quite a lot of debate as to what to prepare! Cooking is a matter of great pride, both personal and nationalistic.

- When the groups have written their menus, ask a spokesperson to read them out, and invite comment and questions from the others.

- The aim of question 2 is to practise some of the input of the unit, that is, quantifiers.

- An interesting way to extend this activity, particularly if you are in an English-speaking environment, is to role-play students doing their shopping in the form of a blocking dialogue. You play the shopkeeper, and as a student asks for something, you present a 'block' which the student has to get round. For example, if a student asks for a pound of potatoes, you can say 'Certainly. Would you like new or old. The new are good scrapers, but the old are best for chipping. Which would you like?' Similarly, if cream is asked for, you can say 'I've only got double and whipping left. Do you want a pint or half a pint?'

● Writing

Aims

- accuracy
- to develop students' awareness of the style of formal and informal letters.

- Students work in pairs to decide which sentences go with which letter, and the correct order.

Answers

Letter to a hotel:
e a l d q k f o
Letter to a friend:
j b h p m c s i n r g
(Students might argue that k. could come after l., and r. after c.)

- The letters are in many ways parallel line for line. Ask students in pairs to compare the different exponents for the same function, one formal and one informal.

Example

Formal *I have a further request.*
Informal *There's something else I'd like to ask you.*

- Students do question 2 in pairs. (See opposite for sample layouts.)

- Students write the two letters. They could begin in class and finish them for homework.

Formal

```
                              47, Angel Road,
                              Blaby,
                              Leicestershire,
                              (date)

The Manager,
Hotel Regent,
107, Carston Square,
London W.1.


Dear Sir,

  ═══════════════════════════════════
  ═══════════════════════════════════
  ═══════════════════════════════════
  ═══════════════════════════════════
  ═══════════════════════════════════
  ═══════════════════════════════════
  ═══════════════════════════════════
  ═══════════════════════════

Yours faithfully,

Chris Bright

Chris Bright
```

Informal

```
                          47, Angel Road,
                          Blaby,
                          Leicestershire.
                          (date)

Dear Jan,

  ～～～～～～～～～～～～～～～～～～
  ～～～～～～～～～～～～～～～～～～
  ～～～～～～～～～～～～～～～～～～
  ～～～～～～～～～～～～～～～～～～
  ～～～～～～～～～～～～～～～～～～
  ～～～～～～～～～～～～～～～～～～
  ～～～～～～～～～～～～～～～～～～
  ～～～～～～～～～～～～～～～～～～
  ～～～～～～～～～～～～～～～～～～
  ～～～～～～～～～～～～～～～～～～
  ～～～～～～～～～～～～～

Love,
(or) Best wishes,

Chris
```

REVISION

Aims

- accuracy
- to revise the forms and concepts of modal verbs introduced in *Headway Intermediate*, in preparation for further work on modals in units 7, 9, 10, and 11 in *Headway Upper-Intermediate*.

- Refer students back to the two letters in the Writing section, and ask them to find the examples of modal verbs and to identify the concept.

  Example

  I'll sleep anywhere.
  Will expresses willingness.

  Could I have a bite to eat . . . ?
  Could expresses permission.

  Could you put me up . . . ?
  Could expresses polite request.

- Students work in groups of three to answer question 1.

  Answers

Can	polite request
can	permission
can't	prohibition
Will	polite request
don't have to	no obligation

- Students read the review of modal verbs, then do question 3 in pairs.

  Answers

a.	1	f.	7
b.	10	g.	19
c.	8	h.	9
d.	16	i.	12
e.	4	j.	5

- For question 4, students work in pairs to prepare a dialogue. When they are ready, ask them to read the dialogues out. You could record some for intensive correction.

UNIT 7

Future forms

What does the future hold?

AIMS OF THE UNIT

- The language input concentrates on forms to express future time, which, for the reasons given below, cause students many problems of form and concept.

- There is a theme of the environment, and First and Third World countries.

- The first Vocabulary section revises and extends the group of nouns and verbs that have the same form, a feature which was introduced in Unit 1, and deals with those pairs which have variable stress (e.g. 'record, to re'cord).

- There is an authentic interview with Jonathon Porritt, the director of Friends of the Earth, which is an environmental pressure group.

NOTES ON THE LANGUAGE INPUT

Future forms

There are two main reasons why foreign students have difficulties in selecting appropriate future forms. Firstly, English has many possible forms to express future time, and secondly, the choice of form depends on *aspect*, that is, how the speaker sees the event, and not on time or certainty.

It has often been said that there is no future tense as such in English. This is because there is no inflected form of the verb used to refer to the future, unlike for example French, Italian, and Spanish. Instead, English has three major forms (**will**, **going to**, and the Present Continuous), and several minor forms (including Present Simple, Future Continuous, and Future Perfect).

Students encounter the following problems:

- They over-use **will**, seeing it as a standard 'future tense' when the pre-arranged nature of verb action requires **going to** or the Present Continuous.

- They resort to a Present Simple/ verb stem 'tense', and use it all the time.

Examples

What you do this weekend?
When you go back to your country?
Where you go on holiday?

- They under-use the Present Continuous to refer to the future, not appreciating its limited but frequent application, i.e. it is used a lot to talk about future arrangements, particularly for the near future, but it is not used for actions that cannot be, or usually are not, arranged.

Examples

It's raining tomorrow.
This is wrong because the weather cannot be arranged.

I'm picking some flowers tonight.
This is wrong because such an event does not require great planning and organization.

NOTES ON THE UNIT
● Discussion point

Aims

- fluency
- free speaking to launch the theme of the future.

- Students work on the Discussion Point in groups. Depending on your students and their interests, each paragraph could provoke long discussion about past, present, and future world situations. Naturally, your students will not always agree with each other.

- Let the discussion go on as long as students are interested. Choose one of the paragraphs that you think is of especial interest to your students for class discussion.

● Reading

Aims

- fluency
- to develop students' reading abilities
- to practise predicting
- to practise identifying topic sentences.

- Answer the first question in the Pre-reading task all together.

- Divide the class into two groups to answer the second question. When the groups have made their lists, compare them all together. This is quite a light-hearted introduction to a rather serious reading text.

- Ask students to read the introduction to the text, then get them to divide into small groups to answer the five questions which follow it. The aim of this is to establish the gist of the article, and to encourage students to make predictions regarding content based on the introduction and the illustration.

Answers

1 *Because it grew of its own accord, and was never formally planned.*
2 *Extreme poverty, overcrowding, pollution, unemployment, disease, inadequate medical care.*
3 *There are rich 'pockets' where the wealthy and powerful people live, and these are probably new, multi-storey blocks of flats.*
4 *Any Third World country.*
5 Students could argue a case for any of the topics being included. None of them are absolutely out of the question, but 'the need for better urban planning' is a little vague and general, and 'the need for birth-control programmes in the Third World' is not directly linked to the problems of 'monster cities'.

- Students scan the article to see which of the topics are discussed. Set a time limit of two minutes. Students discuss in pairs to see if they agree, then read the article in more depth.

- Students work in pairs to answer the Comprehension Check true/false questions.

Answers

1	True	6	True
2	True	7	True
3	False	8	False
4	False	9	True
5	True	10	False

- Answer the 'What do you think?' questions all together. They should provoke a productive discussion.

Answers

1 Students could quote many. First World countries are sometimes known as the North — North America, Russia, Japan, Australia etc. Third World countries are sometimes known as the South —

Central and South America, much of Africa etc.
2 Because the birth rate isn't as high, and there are not as many poor people.
3 Modern industries do not need a large work-force, as machines have replaced them. Examples are the motor industry, agriculture etc.
4 Mexico is brave to try to accommodate so many people. This is a corruption of the title of Aldous Huxley's book 'Brave New World'.
5 There is no set answer.

- Read the introduction about topic sentences all together.
Students work in groups of three to decide what the topic sentences of the first six paragraphs are.

This is quite a difficult exercise, and students might disagree about the sentences. Comprehension, after all, is to a certain extent *subjective*, not *objective*.

Answers

The following are the opinions of the authors.

1 Yes.
2 No. The article is more interested in the future than the past, so *the number . . . will top 3,000 million* is the topic sentence.
3 Yes.
4 This is difficult, as there are two main ideas in the paragraph. i.e. natural population increase is enough to double the population of these cities, without the streams of hopeful migrants as well. The answer is probably 'yes'.
5 No. 'What confronts and confounds urban planners is the enormity of these trends.'
6 Yes.

- Students work in groups to decide what they think the topic sentences are for the remaining paragraphs.

Answers

The following are opinions of the authors.
para. 7 *In the end, both sides agree that the world's biggest cities are mushrooming into the unknown.*

para. 8 *Yet some cities still manage to cope.*
para. 9 *Hong Kong has rehoused 1.3 million people . . .*
para. 10 *. . . despite the dreadful conditions that urban squatters face, their numbers are growing at rates as much as twice those of the cities themselves . . .*
para. 11 *One solution is to ban migration into the cities.*
para. 12 *Mexico City planners are . . . laying plans for a metropolitan region of 36 million people . . .*

- Students work in pairs to practise guessing the meaning of unknown words.

Language focus
Aims

- accuracy
- to compare and contrast different forms used to refer to the future
- to provide controlled practice of **will**, **might**, **going to** and the Present Continuous to refer to the future.

- Read the Language Review all together.

- Sentences for translation (see page iv of the Teacher's Book).

It'll rain tomorrow.
I'll give you my phone number.
He's going to be a pilot when he grows up.
We're getting married in the spring.
The match starts at 3.00.
I'll have dinner at 8.00.
I'll be having dinner at 8.00.
The population will have reached six billion by the year 2000.

- Students read the Grammar section for homework.

- Do the Controlled Practice exercises 1–5. Students work in pairs or small groups.

Answers

1 1 - g. Present Simple to express a fixed time

2 – b. Future Continuous to express activity in progress

3 – a. **Will** to express prediction

4 – e. **Going to** to express intention

5 – d. Present Continuous to express arrangement

6 – h. Future Perfect to express an action finished before a time in the future

7 – c. **Going to** to express a future event based on present evidence

8 – f. **Will** to express spontaneous intention

2 a. **Will** is used to express a decision made on the spur of the moment.
Going to is used because this is already planned and decided.

b. **Will** is used to express a prediction or an intention. The Future Continuous is used to express an activity that will be in progress *around* 8.00.

c. The Present Simple is used to ask about general, week-end habits.
The Present Continous is used to ask about arrangements for the next week-end. Students often over-use the Present Simple to refer to the future, so care needs to be taken with this question.

d. **Will** is used to express a future intention. We know approximately when the action will happen.
The Future Perfect is used to express an action that will have happened *before* tonight.

e. The Present Perfect is used to express an action which began in the past and still continues. The Future Perfect is used to look forward to a time in the future, and to express an action that will have happened before then.

3 Obviously, there are no set answers for this question. Students should be encouraged to ask their own questions.

– Students work in groups of 3 to do question 4.

– Ask them to quickly decide what parts of the country they all work in. Make sure that the parts of the country are quite distant from one another, not just different ends of the same town.

– Students work on their own to fill in the diary, and decide what day would be most convenient, etc.

– For the pair work, ideally the student who is not involved in the telephone conversation should move away to another side of the room, so that he/she cannot hear. This will require careful monitoring of the groups to decide when a phone conversation has ended, and clear instructions.

– Allow adequate time for this question. It is quite challenging, as students are being asked to manipulate several forms to express the future. The forms most probably used are **will**, **going to**, the Present Continuous, and possibly the Present Simple to refer to timetables of trains, planes, etc. Try to correct the phone calls intensively, but don't be disappointed if your students make mistakes. This is a very difficult area of the language, mainly because usage is dictated by aspect.

– You could record some of the phone calls for intensive correction.

– Play the tape in question 5 twice, the second time with students reading the tapescript. The tape includes examples of the major forms used to refer to the future.

● Vocabulary 1

Aims

– accuracy
– to revise and further practise the flexible nature of English vocabulary, where nouns and verbs have the same form
– to introduce students to a group of nouns and verbs having the same form but with variable stress.

– Students were introduced to the flexible nature of English vocabulary in Unit 1. You could remind them of this. The process whereby a word can belong to different classes (e.g. both a verb and an adjective) without the addition of a suffix or a prefix is called conversion, and is extremely prevalent in English. Most word classes can make this change, but the most common is noun and verb the same.

– Read the introduction all together. Students might find it surprising that nouns such as **mushroom** can function as a verb.

– Students do question 1 in pairs or small groups, using dictionaries. Without dictionaries, students would be guessing.

Answers

Verbs and nouns
answer/turn/reply/coach/ design/revolt/cheat/hurry/ notice/paint

Different nouns
solution/arrival/improvement/ agreement

Notice that in some cases there is a slight change in meaning, for example, **to notice** = to see and **a notice** = public piece of news. Also **coach** is a homonym (a person who trains others; a long-distance single-decker bus).

– Students do question 2 in pairs or small groups.

Answers

Nouns and verbs
butter/glue/nurse/arm/question/ judge/experience/experiment/ service/plan

Different verbs
feed/advise/publicize/practise

– Look at the first dictionary entry in question 3 all together. Ask a student to pronounce **increase** as a noun and a verb, and make sure that the class hears the difference. Ask where the stress is on the noun and on the verb.

– Students practise saying the remaining words in pairs, then

practise saying the examples in the entries.
– Read the introduction to question 4 all together. Students use dictionaries to see if the meaning changes.

Answers

The meaning changes in the following words:
object   contract   refuse

– The aim of question 5 is for students to practise *producing* some of the words introduced in questions 3 and 4.

Play the tape, pausing after each unfinished sentence for students to complete using an appropriate word.

Sample answers

1 *Its imports fell by 15 per cent.*
2 *I got a refund.*
3 *Did you get any presents?*
4 *He was convicted of murder.*
5 *I've never been so insulted in all my life!*
6 *Now he's completely addicted.*
7 *We're very pleased with her progress.*
8 *UFO stands for Unidentified Flying Object.*
9 *Three thousand people marched through the streets, protesting about the latest government laws.*
10 *Bella, it gives me great pleasure to present you with this award.*
11 *You need a special permit.*
12 *The governments's latest offer of a 6 per cent pay rise has been rejected by the main teaching union.*

● Listening

Aims

– fluency
– to develop students' listening abilities.

– This is an authentic, unscripted recording, so your students will be challenged, but hopefully they will be sufficiently motivated by the topic to want to listen. Encourage them to 'sit back and enjoy' it, without worrying about parts they do not understand.

– Do the Pre-listening task all together. Encourage discussion at this point on whatever aspects interest your students, perhaps referring to topical issues — for example nuclear power, acid rain, our materialistic society, etc.
– Play the interview in four parts.
Before playing each part, ask students to briefly look at the relevant questions, then close their books. This is because it is both difficult and distracting to listen to a lengthy interview and write notes at the same time.
After each part, students work in pairs or small groups to answer the questions. This way, they can pool their information.

Answers

Part one

1 While he was a teacher, he began to wonder what the future world would be like for the children he was teaching.
2 Because the state of the environment depends on what we as citizens and politicians as decision makers want to do with it.
3 Students might agree or disagree. The point Jonathon Porritt is making is that it is financial considerations that decide most issues, not whether they are 'good' or 'bad'.

Part two

4 A pessimist, because there is a lot to be pessimistic about, and constructive because something must be done about it.
5 *Population.* This will be a big problem in the middle of next century.
The world's resources, both renewable and non-renewable. We are using them up very quickly.
Poverty, famine and hunger in various parts of the world. He thinks this will get worse before the turn of the century.
The arms build-up. One thousand million million dollars are spent every year.

6 Students might agree or disagree. Encourage discussion of this question.

Part three

7 *Awareness.* More people are aware of the need to look after the planet, and are better informed.
Increasing political awareness. People need to involve themselves in organizations.
Awareness of spiritual values or an alternative to materialism, rather than the search for material wealth alone.

Part four

8 He is depressed by the way people treat the planet and each other. But he enjoys his work and the people he works with, and for every example of selfishness and short-sightedness, there are examples of unselfishness.

– Students work in small groups to write a summary of each part of the interview.
– If your students are interested in any of the topics discussed in the interview, they should be motivated to discuss them further.

Language focus

Aims

– accuracy
– to provide students with controlled practice of the Future Perfect and the Future Continuous.

– Students do the Controlled Practice exercises 6 and 7 in pairs or small groups

Answers

6 a. *will have risen*
   b. *will have used up*
   c. *will have found*
   d. *will have replaced*
   e. *will have found*

Students work in pairs to produce some sentences about the planners in Mexico.

Example

They will have built enough houses, schools, and hospitals.
Roads will have been built.

7 7.05 *He'll be standing at the window.*

   7.30 *He'll be getting ready/having a wash.*

   7.45 *He'll be having breakfast.*

   8.30 *He'll be driving to work.*

   8.55 *He'll be climbing the stairs to his office.*

   9.10 *He'll be sitting in his office.*

   1.15 *He'll be having lunch.*

   4.00 *He'll be sitting in his office.*

   6.00 *He'll be driving home.*

Students work in pairs to say what they will be doing at these times tomorrow.

● Speaking

Aims

- fluency
- to provide students with an opportunity for free speaking.

- Students divide into two groups to list past and present problems. When they have finished, ask a spokesperson to read out the lists.
- Students work in pairs to discuss the twentieth century problems. Although this is a serious subject, students will probably approach it with a certain levity as they have the role of optimist/pessimist imposed on them.

● Vocabulary 2

Aims

- accuracy
- to explore synonyms in a text.

- This is the only vocabulary gap-fill exercise in the Students's Book, although there are more in the Workbook. They are naturally very easy to devise, and you might choose to do them more often. Cloze tests and gap-fill exercises are called global tests, because they are not just testing discrete items, but a wide range of skills. Students need to understand the *content* of the text, the *style*, the *structures* and *vocabulary*; they need to be able to identify the *part of speech* of the missing item; and they need to

appreciate the writer's intention. These are the skills involved in finding a suitable word to fill each gap.

- In a pure Cloze test, every nth word is blanked out, usually every seventh. Thus there is a random selection of words that students must put in. In this gap-fill exercise, selected words have been blanked out to explore the possibility of synonyms. It is often said that there are no true synonyms in English, i.e. no two words have exactly the same meaning and connotations. This is true according to dictionary definitions, but often in a text several words could be substituted, and this is one of the aims of this exercise. In the answers, the word that appeared in the original text is given first, followed by acceptable alternatives. These should be discussed with your students by asking questions such as 'What's the difference between the two words? Which one is stronger/better/more appropriate?'

- An interesting way to approach this exercise is for students to work first in pairs to fill the gaps, then in groups of four, then as a class, to compare their answers and to discuss alternatives. Finally you go through it with them, correcting and discussing the various possibilities.

Answers

1 *struggle, fight*
2 *suffer*
3 *care, treatment, attention*
4 *contact, interaction*
5 *nearby (Together is grammatically possible, but does not fit the main point of the paragraph.)*
6 *participation, participating, involvement*
7 *rather*
8 *sense, feeling*
9 *dictated, determined, decided*
10 *presented*
11 *symbols, signs*
12 *indoors, inside*
13 *wander*
14 *floors, storeys*
15 *counted, depended, relied*

- The article presents a different view of the Third World from that in the Reading and Listening sections, and could provide stimulus for a productive discussion.

The article is particularly well written. For example the artificiality of work in First World countries is well expressed by the phrase 'make money mysteriously appear in banks', and the third paragraph is nicely constructed to contrast what the child in the Third World does for real and what the child in the First World does for play.

● Writing

Aims

- accuracy
- to help students with discursive writing, by means of work on clauses of concession and discourse markers of opinion.

- Write on the board the following two sentences:

  It was raining.
  We played tennis.

  Ask students in pairs to combine the sentences to make one sentence in as many ways as they can.

- Students do questions 1–4 in pairs or small groups.

Answers

1 *I tried to ring you yesterday, but you weren't in.*
   We had a good game of tennis despite the rain.
   Thank you for your invitation. However, I am afraid I cannot come.
   I went to work although I was not feeling well.
   Beethoven was deaf from the age of forty. Nevertheless, he continued to compose music.

This is a difficult area to explain, and it should be approached under two headings, 'concept' and 'use'. Naturally, all of the linking devices express a contrast of ideas. **But** expresses the weakest contrast and **nevertheless** the strongest. Sentences with **but** can usually be expressed with **although** too, but note that **but** cannot come at the beginning of a sentence while **although** can come at the beginning and in the middle. The contrast is stronger with **although**.

Examples

She worked hard, but she failed the exam.
Although she worked hard, she failed the exam.
She failed the exam, although she worked hard.

Despite is followed by a noun. **However** usually comes at the beginning of a sentence and is followed by a comma. **Nevertheless** is the same, but is more literary and formal.

It is worth pointing out to students that the best way to learn this area is by practice rather than studying the rules.

There are no set answers for questions 2 and 3.

4 a. *personally*
   b. *That is why*
   c. *Generally speaking*
   d. *Obviously*
   e. *What is more*

- Read through the introduction to question 5 all together.
- Students begin to write the essay of their choice in class, and finish it for homework.

REVISION

Aims

- accuracy
- to introduce students to the use of **so** and **not** after verbs of opinion.

- This is a very common structure, which causes students several problems of form.

Common mistakes

A Is Peter coming to the party?
B *I think.
    *I think no.
    *I think he isn't.

This last mistake is particularly common. When expressing a

negative opinion introduced by think, English prefers to put the negative with think, i.e. *I don't think he is.*

This Revision section aims to highlight these areas, but the best way to teach and learn them is by being vigilant in the course of normal classroom interaction and picking up students' mistakes.

- Read question 1 all together.
- Students do question 2 in pairs. There are no set answers.
- Students do question 3 in pairs. Point out that the questions must be inverted, not **wh-** type.

Example

Are you going on holiday this year? (Not *Where are you going on holiday?*)

UNIT 8

Description

Our colourful world

AIMS OF THE UNIT

- The function of describing is, of course, a very wide area. In the unit on Descriptions in *Headway Intermediate*, the focus was on asking for descriptions (**What . . . like?; What . . . look like?**) and comparative and superlative adjectives and adverbs. In *Headway Upper-Intermediate*, the focus is on giving descriptions, and the topics include describing people's appearance and life-style, a landscape, a meal, and the seasons.

- The Writing section concentrates on describing a city for two different purposes, one factual and one persuasive.

- The grammatical input consists of three structures commonly used in the giving of descriptions; relative clauses, participle clauses, and modifying adverbs.

- In the Revision section, students are introduced to the many different uses of the verb **get**, and there is the first of three exercises in the approach to multi-word verbs (or phrasal verbs) in the Student's Book. See page 51 of the Teacher's Book for more detail.

NOTES ON THE LANGUAGE INPUT

Relative clauses

This is an area which students are often quite conversant with on a superficial level, but closer investigation reveals problems of form. In defining relative clauses, several forms are possible, but there is usually one that sounds best to an English ear; students confuse the relative pronouns used in defining and non-defining relative clauses and, where possible, relative pronouns are dropped.

Common mistakes

*That's the woman who she bought my car.
*People which work in banks earn a lot of money.
*The man to who I spoke was the manager.
*The house which I liked best was the first one which we saw.

In this last example, English would prefer to drop both relative pronouns to form contact clauses.

You should stress to your students that defining relative clauses are much more common than non-defining, the latter usually being found written rather than spoken.

Participle clauses

Participles used as adjectives should be familiar to students at this level, but you can still expect some mistakes such as *I'm interesting in jazz*. On a more complex level, the use of participles is hard to analyse. As Swan says in *Practical English Usage*, 'It is not always easy to explain why one participle can be used before a noun (e.g. a lost dog), but another one cannot (e.g. a found object).'

However, this is not an area which students frequently confront.

The correct use of participle clauses by your students would show quite an instinctive grasp of English, as they are examples of a refined style of language use. Students may be unconsciously translating them from their own language, but it is unlikely that you could 'teach' them for productive purposes.

Modifying adverbs

Generally speaking, modifying adverbs cause students few problems because they do not try to use them much, restricting themselves to **very** and **quite**, plus whatever adjectives they might know. The more ambitious students may try to sound 'English' and use **really, awfully, absolutely,** etc., probably with mixed success. It is an interesting area to point out to students, as it can greatly enhance their ability to be precise and descriptive.

Unfortunately, this too is a complex area of English. The distinction between limit and gradable adjectives does not always exist; for example, we can say both *She's very beautiful* and *She's absolutely beautiful*. Also the use of modifying adverbs + limit adjective seems to be dictated by collocation (i.e. words that go together) rather than any definable rule.

Nevertheless, it is worth encouraging students to be more ambitious in their use of modifiers, even if this might include some errors.

NOTES ON THE UNIT

● Discussion point

Aims

- fluency
- to launch the theme of descriptions, and to test students' abilities in describing a landscape.

- Answer question 1 all together, and encourage as much discussion as possible with your questions.

Examples

Why do you think it's that country?
Are you sure?
Where else could it be?

Naturally, guessing the correct country is less important than a good justification and description. The pictures were chosen to slightly mislead students.

Answers

The Seychelles (beach scene)
Switzerland (mountain stream)
Japan (lake in mountains)
Kenya (village)

(Students should guess the time of year.)

- Students work in pairs to write the postcard. Allow adequate time, perhaps 15–20 minutes, for the pairs to get some ideas together and start writing, for you to go round correcting, and finally to have the postcards all read out. Stress that you want more than just one or two sentences – quite a long postcard, in fact!

● Reading

Aims

- fluency
- to develop students' reading abilities, and their appreciation of an English writer.

- Somerset Maugham is famous for his portrayals of exotic people and places, which he describes in fine detail. The extracts in this section were chosen because they include descriptions of a person, a meal and its setting, and a person's life-style.

Together with the résumés, they tell the whole short story, and it is a tale which is typical of Maugham – the escape from the ordinary and the monotonous, but at a price. Students might be inspired to read further stories of his, and they would certainly be making a good choice.

Read the introduction all together. Your students might like to know that he was born in 1874 and died in 1965, and this story was written in the 1920s.

Check students' understanding of 'boldly taken the course of his own life into his own hands'. It means that he has done something to take charge of his life, in a way, presumably, that not many of us do.

- Students read the extracts and answer the Comprehension Check questions. Don't encourage students to ask you about the meaning of unknown words, but naturally, if an item is causing problems, then you should help. Immediately before students read the next extract (and after the résumé), ask students to predict what might come next.

Answers

1 His physical appearance, including face, clothes, and the impression he creates. The description is sympathetic, but closely critical.
2 As his clothes were 'suitable to the place and the weather' and he is 'deeply sunburned', he has probably been there for a long time.
3 Obviously, the artistic quality of your students' sketches is unimportant. This question should be treated quite light-heartedly, and also quite quickly.
4 Night is approaching, so it is perhaps between 8.00 and 9.00 in the evening. We have the impression it is a small, country inn, very quiet and pretty in an unsophisticated way. It is a family inn. The food is simple but of excellent quality. The wine was light and refreshing. The atmosphere is intimate, relaxed, and romantic. The two

men settle down to a meal, with plenty of wine in an attractive setting and with the prospect of a long conversation ahead.
5 Because they have just finished their second bottle of wine! They are getting a little drunk.
6 He thinks that work should be a means to enjoying yourself, and not done for its own sake.
7 He means the moon looks the same, it is the same size. The writer interprets Wilson's comment literally, and points out somewhat pedantically that it is of course the same moon.
8 The light was only just bright enough to eat by, but it is just right for intimate exchanges.
9 He is special because of the way he has taken control of his life and because of what he intends to do when his income runs out. In every other respect (his appearance, his life-style, his likes) he is absolutely ordinary.
10 Because of the contrast between the way Wilson began his life and the way he has chosen to end it; because such an ordinary man could make such an awful decision, and because, unlike most people, he has found happiness.

- Answer the 'What do you think?' questions all together. This could easily develop into a productive discussion, as the short story makes people wonder about the way they have chosen to lead their lives.

Language focus

Aims

- accuracy
- to provide students with controlled practice of relative clauses and participle clauses, and to practise building complex sentences.

- Read the Language Review all together.

- Sentences for translation (see page iv of the Teacher's Book).

What's the name of the man who discovered penicillin?

45

A cork-screw is an instrument that is used for opening bottles.
The man you met yesterday was my father.
That's the man whose dog bit me.
I met a woman riding a donkey.
He went to the party dressed as a policeman.

- Students read the Grammar section in class.
- Do the Controlled Practice exercises 1–4.
  Students do exercises 1–3 in pairs or small groups.

Answers

1 a. *who*
  b. *where*
  c. *nothing*
  d. *who*
  e. *whose*
  f. *that* (If there was a comma after *pension*, it would be a non-defining relative clause, and *which* would be possible. This is a very fine point, and not worth going into too deeply.)
  g. *that*
  h. *where*
  i. *nothing*
  j. *nothing*

2 a. *I read a book which/that was written by a friend of yours.*
     I read a book written by a friend of yours.
  b. *A man, who was carrying a monkey in a box, got on the bus.*
     A man carrying a monkey in a box got on the bus.
  c. *In the street there were several people who were waiting for the shop to open.*
     In the street there were several people waiting for the shop to open.
  d. *Britain imports many cars which/that are made in Japan.*
     Britain imports many cars made in Japan.
  e. *There are a lot of people in your office who want to talk to you.*
     There are a lot of people in your office wanting to talk to you.

  f. *The cowboy, who was wounded by an arrow, fell off his horse.*
     The cowboy, wounded by an arrow, fell off his horse.
  g. *Most of the people who were injured in the crash recovered quickly.*
     Most of the people injured in the crash recovered quickly.
  h. *John, who wished he hadn't come to the party, looked anxiously at his watch.*
     Wishing he hadn't come to the party, John looked anxiously at his watch.
     Or, alternatively
     John looked anxiously at his watch, wishing he hadn't come to the party.

3 a. *Peter, who works in London for a firm that sells computers, has a three-bedroomed house overlooking the Thames.*
  b. *An elderly man with a wrinkled face, wearing an old raincoat, walked slowly along the dusty, tree-lined road.*
  c. *Ann Cross, the actress who won an Oscar for a film made last year, was seen in a restaurant having dinner with a man whose company recently went bankrupt.*

- Students work in five groups to see who can make the longest sentence. Expect some groups to produce modest results, whilst others will make extraordinarily long and complex sentences, often of a humorous nature.

- There are exercises in the Workbook on all the above areas.

● Vocabulary 1

Aims

- accuracy
- to introduce students to a set of vocabulary to describe people, including compound adjectives.

- Students work in pairs or small groups to answer questions 1–4.

Answers

1 Clothes
  not ironed = *creased*
  not buttoned up = *open at the neck*
  attractive and colourful = *picturesque*
  Face
  a soft smile = *a gentle smile*
  wrinkled = *lined*
  brown = *sunburned*
  ordinary = *plain*
  Hair
  neat = *carefully brushed*
  Character
  thinking of oneself = *selfish*
  having experience and knowledge = *wise*
  ordinary = *commonplace*

2 Character
  bad-tempered/well-behaved/narrow-minded/easy-going/self-centred
  Clothes
  well-dressed
  Face
  good-looking/blue-eyed/clean-shaven
  Body
  left-handed/straight-haired/broad-shouldered

3 a. *He isn't very tall.*
  b. *Her hair isn't very tidy.*
  c. *She doesn't look very happy.*
  d. *He isn't very polite/nice/kind.*
  e. *He hasn't got a very nice complexion.*
  f. *She isn't very well-dressed.*
  g. *I don't think he looks very clever.*

4 From left to right: *Henry, Daniel, Emily, James, Robert* (standing), *Grannie* (sitting), *Alice, Clare.*

- Students work in four groups to describe one of the pictures. The aim is partly for students to practise the words they have just learned, but also for them to ask you or their colleagues for other words they need to describe the people, so encourage them to do this.

46

● Speaking

Aims

- fluency
- to provide students with an opportunity for free speaking.

- Students giving short prepared talks is a most useful activity for this level, and you might choose to do it often at other points in the book. Generally, students approach the task quite conscientiously, and talk about topics that are personal and interesting. What is nice is that discussion often ensues, and question and answer forms are practised in a genuine interaction between all the members of the class, including yourself.

  For some of your students, it might be an important aspect of their job to be able to give presentations that are clear, logical and well-organized, and you might like to give these students feedback on their performance of the task, as well as their linguistic ability.

  To have all the members of your class giving lecturettes in the same lesson will probably be undesirable, unless you have a small class. One approach is to have either one or two students giving their lecturette each day, spread over however many days this requires. Put the days and who is to speak on that day on your notice board, and remind students in advance when it is their turn.

  It is important that students do not read out from their notes, as this then becomes an exercise in reading aloud, not speaking, and few people are good at reading aloud in their first language, let alone in a second language. Encourage the speaker to direct his/her talk at all the class, not just you.

  You might choose to make notes of language mistakes, picking up on general areas, or areas you have recently been working on; alternatively, you could choose to just let the activity go through. It might be inhibiting if students feel their performance is being in any

way assessed, and the attraction of this activity is the genuineness of the interaction.

● Listening

Aims

- fluency
- to develop students' listening abilities.

- Do the Pre-listening task all together if you have a small class, or in groups if you have a large class. Encourage as much discussion as possible.
- Students listen to the tape and take notes. Let them compare notes in pairs. You might, or might not, choose to replay the tape.
- Students do the Comprehension Check questions in pairs.

Answers

1 table with food and drink – he had been sitting outside having a meal on this particular day.

man with painful jaw – his jaw froze in the cold weather later the same day.

skis – people were going up the mountain to ski.

car with broken windscreen – the car which finally gave him a lift.

brandy – he had one or two to help him thaw out.

snow-plough – they had been out pushing snow into the middle of the road.

sandals – he was wearing sandals in the snow.

mountain village – the villages he went through while it was snowing.

people laughing – they didn't believe his story.

2 Students re-tell the story in pairs or small groups.

Language focus

Aims

- accuracy
- to provide students with practice in recognizing and producing modifying adverbs.

- Students are asked to recognize a range of modifiers in the exercises, but to produce only two, **very** and **absolutely**. This is because of the problems of collocation mentioned in the introduction to this unit.
- Play the tape again, and ask students to fill in the modifiers.

Answers

1 *very*	5 *extremely*
2 *quite*	6 *awfully*
3 *really*	7 *absolutely*
4 *rather*	8 *quite*

- Read the Language Review all together.
- Sentences for translation (see page iv of the Teacher's Book).

  The meal was very good.
  The meal was absolutely wonderful.
  I feel extremely tired.
  I feel completely exhausted.

- Students read the Grammar section in class or for homework.
- Do the Controlled Practice exercise 5.
  Students work in pairs to prepare their dialogues.
  After a while, ask some of them to repeat their dialogues for the class to hear.
- There is an exercise in the Workbook that provides further practice in this area.

● Vocabulary 2

Aims

- accuracy
- to introduce students to a set of vocabulary to describe colours, shapes, and materials.

- Students do question 1 in pairs or small groups.

Answers

Shape
circular/cylindrical/straight/oval/round/triangular/rectangular/square.

Material
gold/rubber/cotton/nylon/glass/wooden/metal/silver/iron.

Colour
gold/grey/scarlet/purple/crimson/silver/navy blue/maroon/turquoise.

- Do question 2 all together. Expect some argument about colour, as not everyone agrees on certain colours.
- Students do question 3 in pairs. As they are preparing, go round checking the accuracy of their descriptions as, if they are too full of errors, it is very difficult for the rest of the class to understand, and this would spoil the activity.

● Writing

Aims

- accuracy
- to develop students' awareness of the writer's purpose, and to distinguish fact and opinion.

- As a lead-in to this activity, you could divide the class into two groups and ask them to write a factual description of the town you are in, and an advertisement to attract tourists or business.
- Students read the two descriptions, and answer the questions at the end.

Answers

1 The purpose of the first text is to give factual information about the history, amenities, etc. of Cardiff. The purpose of the second is to attract business and tourists.

   The first is taken from an encyclopaedia, and the second from publicity issued by the Welsh Development Agency.

2 The first is more factual. The style of the second is more subjective, and personal. It is more colourful and may be exaggerated.

3 First: introduction; geographical location
   Second: the lay-out of the city; its major buildings; its industry and transport
   Third: its history up to the present day

4 This is a thought-provoking question, as different parts of the same phrase may be fact or opinion.

Example

one of the world's great civic centres.

- Students begin to write their descriptions in class, and finish them for homework.

REVISION

Aims

- accuracy
- to practise the many uses of the verb **get**
- to do a preparatory exercise on multi-word verbs, which are dealt with in depth in the next unit.

- **Get** is one of the most common verbs in spoken English, and it is unlikely that your students are using it to express the various concepts illustrated in sentences a. to h. in question 1. They are much more likely to use the words underneath (**fetch, catch, buy**, etc.).
- Students do questions 1–3 in pairs.

Answers

1 a. *arrived*   e. *earns*
   b. *buy*   f. *fetch*
   c. *becoming*   g. *have/buy*
   d. *catching*   h. *receive*

2 a. *back*   e. *over*
   b. *in*   f. *out, off*
   c. *away, out*   g. *off*
   d. *past, by*   h. *through to*

3 **Sample answers**
   a. *The burglar managed to get in by breaking a window.*
   b. *. . . but the burglar got away before they arrived.*
   c. *Naturally we got out as quickly as possible.*
   d. *We didn't get back until three in the morning.*
   e. *. . . but I got it out.*
   f. *I've been trying to get through to you for ages, . . .*

- Question 4 is the first general exercise in *Headway Upper-Intermediate* on multi-word verbs. For an explanation of the approach to this difficult area of the language, see page 51 in the next unit of the Teacher's Book.

- Students work in pairs to complete the sentences.
   If they have problems, try through mime and acting to show the logic behind the choice of adverb/ preposition.

Answers

   a. *down*   h. *in*
   b. *away/off*   i. *off*
   c. *out, away/off* j. *up*
   d. *away*   k. *off*
   e. *out*   l. *down*
   f. *in*   m. *down*
   g. *off, on*   n. *out*

There is a progress test on the first eight units of *Headway Upper-Intermediate* in the Workbook.

UNIT 9

Modal verbs of deduction

Relationships

AIMS OF THE UNIT

- Modal verbs express five broad areas of meaning: obligation, ability, permission, volition, and certainty/uncertainty. Of these, the first four were introduced in *Headway Intermediate* and revised in the Revision section of Unit 6, *Headway Upper-Intermediate*. This unit concentrates on the final area.

- The Vocabulary sections deal with the complex areas of multi-word verbs and understanding idiomatic expressions.

- There is a jigsaw reading activity on the subject of parent – child relationships.

- The Writing section revises reported speech.

NOTES ON THE LANGUAGE INPUT

Modal verbs of certainty and uncertainty

Modal verbs to express degrees of certainty about the future were dealt with in Unit 7. This deals with certainty about the present and the past.

The use of **must** and **can't** + Present or Perfect infinitive presents students with no great problems of concept, as similar forms and use exist in many languages. However, students rarely use **might** or **could** + Present or Perfect infinitive to express possibility, as there is no comparable form in their language. Instead they tend to use **perhaps**, which is much easier to manipulate but not at all English.

Common mistakes

*Perhaps I'll see you later.
(I might see you later.)

*Perhaps he's having a bath.
(He might be having a bath.)

*Perhaps they got lost.
(They could have got lost.)

For this reason, material in the Students' Book and the Workbook tries to force students to use neglected modals, and you, too, should be vigilant in encouraging them to explore this area.

NOTES ON THE UNIT

● Discussion point

Aims
- fluency
- to launch the theme of the unit
- to test students' abilities in using modal verbs of deduction.

- You could launch this activity by brainstorming words for members of the family. Naturally students will know **brother, father**, etc., but ask them to explore the relatives one acquires when one marries, not forgetting when the marriage is to a divorced person (e.g. **mother-in-law, stepson**).

- Students talk in small groups to try to decide how the people in the photograph are related.

Naturally, the task is not to *know* how they are all related, but to discuss the different possibilities, so if students immediately say *That's his wife, and they are his parents*, encourage them to use **must** by asking *Are you sure?*, and encourage them too to speculate about other possible relationships, e.g. *He could be her brother because they've both got blond hair, or he might be her brother-in-law*. They are, in fact, related in the following way:

The man (1) and woman (2) holding children are husband and wife, and the children (3 and 4), both girls, are theirs. The older man (5) and woman (6) are 1's parents, therefore 2's in-laws and the grandparents of 3 and 4. The man with the moustache (7) is married to 1's sister, so is brother-in-law to 1 and 2, and the boy at the back is 7's son. The person who took the photograph is 1's sister, 7's wife.

- The task is similar for question 2. Again, encourage students to use the modal verbs of deduction. If they say *This one is from a newspaper*, ask *Are you sure?*.

Answers

1 From the problem page of a magazine.
A wife wrote in complaining about her husband's behaviour. The relationship doesn't sound very good. He seems to be out a lot, while she is stuck at home.

2 From *The Times* Court and Social page, written by either Malcolm's or Penelope's parents. They are obviously upper-middle class. You could point out the double-barrelled names.

3 From the wedding ceremony in the Book of Common Prayer. You could point out that the woman has the option of saying 'to obey' or not.

4 This will probably be the hardest for students. They might be able to work out that it comes from a diary, and that it was written by a teenager complaining about his parents' behaviour, but the humour will probably escape them. They might be able to deduce that the child is about fifteen or sixteen years old, and that he is in love! The extract comes from *The Secret Diary of Adrian Mole* by Susan Townsend.

– You could encourage discussion at this point about any of the topics mentioned in the Discussion Point.

Example

Do you come from a big family?
How close are you?
Are you an uncle/aunt?
Do people announce their engagement in the papers in your country?
What are the wedding vows?

● Reading

Aims

– fluency
– to develop students' reading abilities, especially inference
– to provide an opportunity for free speaking, as this is a jigsaw activity.

– Students divide into two groups, those with children and those without. Depending on the age of your students, you might not have any parents in the class, or only one or two, but this doesn't matter. If there is just one student with children, you could go and talk to him/her yourself.

Let the discussion go on for as long as students are interested, i.e. about

10 to 12 minutes. They could well want to know the meaning of the multi-word verbs (**take after, bring up**) and they might need reminding of the structure *Who are you like?*

– Students divide up to read the two versions of the relationship. It is unlikely that you will have an equal division of parents and non-parents, and for the sake of a jigsaw you need this, so move students to whichever side is necessary. For the reading, it doesn't really matter who reads which part, parent or non-parent.

– Students read one version. Make sure they *don't* read the wrong version, *or* both versions. Either of these would spoil the rest of the activity.

– In their groups they discuss answers to the Comprehension Check questions. These were designed to exercise students' powers of inferencing, and very few of them require direct reference to the text. Students might reach a certain agreement in their answers, but it doesn't matter if they disagree as long as they can justify their opinions.

– When students have discussed all the questions in their groups, they split up to talk to a member of the other group, and compare their answers.

Answers

Questions 1–3 were designed to provoke different interpretations of the relationship, and students will have varying information in answer to questions 4–10.

– The text and the questions were designed to prompt practice in modal verbs of deduction (e.g. *They might have been closer when Amy was a child, because he says he thinks it's a lovely age for a child*), but don't necessarily expect this to happen, and don't interrupt to impose the language but rather let students get on with the reading and speaking. There should be a lot of talking at this point, as students compare their own interpretations of the relationship. There are no set

answers to these Comprehension Check questions, as students' understanding of the relationship, its closeness, and its problems, are very subjective.

Sample answers (in the authors' opinions)

1 c. is perhaps best. James would argue that their relationship was closer when she was young, but Amy would say she didn't see much of him. He would say she is his best friend, but she would say that she doesn't really know him. It's probably true to say they don't have much in common.

2 b. is perhaps best. James would say that he has done everything he can to help, and Amy would say that he is selfish, but he doesn't really seem to be able to understand her.

3 b. is perhaps the most true; a. is certainly possible; c. is a little extreme but not entirely wrong.

4 He thought they were strange, and came and disappeared quickly.

5 He thinks she must have upset somebody; she says she was asked to leave.

6 She says it was because they weren't challenging enough, and she probably didn't know what she wanted to do; he probably thinks she gave up too quickly and was impulsive.

7 He probably doesn't like him because he isn't famous. In James's version, what is significant is that he doesn't say anything about his son-in-law.

8 No.

9 No.

10 Not often.

– Answer the 'What do you think?' question all together. This could develop into a productive discussion, not only about the Mitfords but also about parent/child relationships generally.

Language focus

Aims

– accuracy
– to provide students with controlled practice of modal verbs of deduction.

- Read the Language Review all together.
- Sentences for translation (see page iv of the Teacher's Book).

He must be at least sixty.
She can't have grandchildren. She's too young.
They might be asleep. There are no lights on.
She must be working hard at the moment. She looks tired.
They must have got lost. They're very late.
They can't have remembered how to get here.
Their car might have broken down.
They can't have been looking where they were going.

- Students read the Grammar section in class.

- Do the Controlled Practice exercises 1 and 2.
Students do the exercises in pairs or small groups.

Answers

1 The sentences to be rewritten in this exercise force students to use a modal verb of deduction, and there is little choice. The reasons to support their deductions are of the students' choice so only sample answers can be given here.
   a. *She can't like children very much. She doesn't want any.*
   b. *James must be a famous actor. He's often on the television and has won an award.*
   c. *She might have a farm. She likes the countryside very much.*
   d. *She can't have worked very hard at school. She had to leave.*
   e. *James might have won an Oscar. He's won several awards.*
   f. *She must have had a lot of friends when she was young. Her father said a lot of people came to their house.*
   g. *He can't have wanted her to marry Gerald. He tried to break them up.*
   h. *He must have wanted her to marry someone famous. He's a bit of a snob.*

   i. *They can't be very close to each other. They don't see each other very often.*
   j. *She might get on better with her mother. She doesn't seem to like her father very much.*

2 **Sample answers**
   a. *They might be having a party/a row.*
   b. *He/she might have overslept/might be doing the photocopying.*
   c. *She must have been making a lot of phone calls.*
   d. *He must be on a diet./He might have been doing some exercise.*
   e. *He/she might have been drinking/might have had a heart attack.*

● Vocabulary 1

Aims

- accuracy
- to introduce students to the system of multi-word verbs.

- The term multi-word verb is gaining in popularity because it avoids the problem of whether the particle is an adverb or a preposition. From a grammarian's point of view, this is important, but from a student's point of view, the distinction is irrelevant.

Grammarians generally agree that there are four types of multi-word verb, but differ in their terminology (they are also called compound verbs). Broadly speaking, given that a preposition must be followed by an object, those multi-word verbs that are followed by an object and where the particle cannot come after the object are prepositional verbs. Those multi-word verbs that either have no object, or where the particle can come after the object, are phrasal verbs. Those verbs followed

by two particles, one a preposition and one an adverb, are called phrasal-prepositional verbs.

In *Headway Upper-Intermediate*, and in many other course books and grammars, the following four types are identified:

Type 1
Verb + adverb (Phrasal verb without an object)
Example
The plane took off.

Type 2
Verb + adverb + object (Phrasal verb + adverb + object)
Example
I turned the light on.
Here the particle can come after the object, if it is not a pronoun. This is the most common type.

Type 3
Verb + preposition + object (Prepositional verb)
Example
My wife looks after the bills.

Type 4
Verb + adverb + preposition + object (Phrasal-prepositional verb)
Example
I'm looking forward to my holiday.

- The problems that students face in both understanding multi-word verbs and using them accurately are well-known. The most common verbs, of whatever type, are easily acquired through constant exposure. Students use, happily and relatively correctly, multi-word verbs such as the following:

I got up at seven.
The plane took off.
(Type 1)

She put on her hat.
He turned the television on.
(Type 2)

What are you talking about?
I'll look after your cat.
(Type 3)

I get on very well with my parents.
I'm looking forward to the weekend.
(Type 4)

This is an area of the language where it might well be argued that 'ignorance is bliss'. Confronting students formally and comprehensively with the rules of form and concept could well depress rather than reassure, and it needs to be approached with care and sensitivity. On a more positive note, it is the opinion of the authors that one extremely digestible aspect of multi-word verbs is frequently ignored, and that is when both the verb and the particle carry their literal meanings. There are many thousands of examples, and drawing students' attention to at least a few of them not only makes the area seem less daunting, but can help students begin to 'feel' the element of meaning that the particle adds to to the verb.

- In *Headway Upper-Intermediate*, therefore, there is a three-stage approach to multi-word verbs:

1 An introduction to their literal use (in the Revision section of Unit 8 and a remedial exercise at the beginning of this Vocabulary section).
2 An introduction to the use of the particle as intensifier of the verb meaning.
3 An introduction to their non-literal use.

In addition, there is an exercise on the non-literal use of multi-word verbs in Unit 9 of the Workbook, an exercise on Type 4 multi-word verbs in Unit 10 of the Workbook, and an introduction to nouns formed from multi-word verbs in Unit 12 of the Student's Book.

- The authors feel that the problems students encounter in the use of non-literal multi-word verbs have been underestimated. Not only must they know the form (what type it is) and the meaning (which is often very subtle) but they must know what it collocates with. For example, one can talk about **taking up a sport, a job** or **a hobby**, but one cannot **take up a boyfriend, dieting**, or **going to bed early**. This problem is such that *The Oxford Dictionary of Current Idiomatic English* Volume 1 on *Verbs with Prepositions and*

Particles lists common collocations in each entry.

---

take up³ [B1iii pass] adopt as a pastime. **O:** gardening, golf, stamp-collecting □ *I should have taken up singing — everybody used to tell me so.* TOH □ *Why not take up some outdoor sport as a relaxation from office work?*
take up⁴ [B1iii pass] start a job, begin work. **O:** office, employment, one's duties □ *I would be required on taking up my duties in Whitehall to give my views and assist in making decisions.* MFM □ *Charley threw up his job to take up more respectable, more sensible employment.* BFA
take up⁵ [B1i pass] take as a protégé, patronize. **S:** impresario, actor-manager, conductor. **O:** (promising, young) singer, actor, soloist □ *A young actor will find it hard to make his way on the London stage unless he is exceptionally talented or has someone established to take him up.*
take up⁶ [B1i pass] join in, add one's voice to. **O:** song, chant; chorus, refrain □ *It was Pop who started the song, and everyone took it up in shrill voices.* DBM □ *Someone started to sing 'For he's a jolly good fellow,' and the chorus was taken up by all the others.* PE
take up⁷ [B1iii pass] continue a story which has been interrupted, or left unfinished by someone else; pick up ¹⁵ (q v). **O:** tale, story; (narrative) thread □ *He takes up the tale at the outbreak of war in 1939.* NM □ *We were back at our posts again and Ned was taking up the thread. Even Randall was listening.* CON
take up⁸ [B1i pass] raise, mention, a topic in order to consider or discuss it. **O:** question, matter, issue, point □ *Much in the story has interesting parallels to the present time. I shall not take these up, however.* SNP □ *There are one or two points of detail that should be taken up before we move on.*

- For these reasons, students are expected to do the following in *Headway Upper-Intermediate*.

1 Recognize and produce those multi-word verbs that are used literally.
2 Recognize and begin to produce those multi-word verbs where the particle is used to intensify the verb meaning.
3 Perceive the system of the non-literal use of multi-word verbs, produce the most common of these, and recognize a greater number.

It is often said that a student's ability to use multi-word verbs accurately and appropriately in English is a true sign of mastery of the language, but the authors feel that such proficiency is acquired at a considerably more advanced level than upper-intermediate, if ever.

- Ask your students to read the Grammar section on multi-word verbs for homework before

beginning this lesson, and tell them not to worry if they don't understand it all!

- Remind students of the exercise they did in the Revision section of Unit 8. You could mime some of the actions and ask students to tell you what you are doing.

Example
You're blowing up a balloon.
You fell off the chair.
You're writing down a telephone number.

- Students work in pairs to think of a reply to the following questions with a multi-word verb used literally:

What do you do with a magazine picture that you want to keep?
What do you do with a tree that is in the way?
What do you do with rubbish and kitchen waste?
What does a dustman do with your rubbish?
What do you do with a cat at night?
What do you have to do with a dog two or three times a day?
What should you do with a library book that you've finished reading?
How do you replace a broken light bulb?

- You could ask students to work in groups of four to check their answers. Don't expect them to have all the answers correct. Even though the verbs and particles are being used literally, they still cause problems. Students' suggestions can often be very funny; for example, a dentist 'pulls up' or 'knocks in' teeth; you 'take off/away/in' a library book that you've finished reading. Again, you could mime their incorrect suggestions to highlight their literal meaning.

- Read the introduction to question 2 all together. Students work in pairs to put one of the particles into each gap.

Answers

a.	*up*	g.	*down*
b.	*up*	h.	*up*
c.	*up*	i.	*out*
d.	*out*	j.	*up*
e.	*out*	k.	*down*
f.	*down*	l.	*up*

- In exercise 3, students work in groups of four to compare the use of multi-word verbs in each pair of sentences.

The sentences were chosen to highlight the problems of form and use.

Those students who have been introduced to this area previously will probably spot the problems, whilst other students might not see any particular problem at all.

The following points might emerge:

a. *He looked up the chimney* is literal. 'Up' is a preposition.
   He looked the word up is non-literal.
   Sometimes the same verb + particle has different meanings, and belongs to different types.

b. *She put out the cat* is literal.
   She put out her cigarette is non-literal.
   Sometimes the same verb + particle has different meanings and belongs to the same type.

c. With some multi-word verbs the particle can move. *Look after* is not one of these.

d. *The plane took off* is non-literal and does not take an object.
   He took off his coat is literal and takes an object.

e. *She came across the room* is literal.
   I came across this old photograph is non-literal.
   Sometimes the same verb + particle has different meanings and belongs to the same type.

- Ask students to identify those sentences where the adverb can move position, by saying the sentences out loud and seeing if they 'sound right'.

The adverb can move in the following sentences:

He looked up the word in the dictionary. (He looked the word up . . .)
She put the cat out, locked the door and went to bed. (She put out the cat . . .)
She put her cigarette out in the ash-tray. (She put out her cigarette . . .)

He took his coat off. (He took off his coat.)

- You might choose to do the remaining questions on multi-word verbs in another lesson. Students and teacher could well want a break!

- Students work in pairs to do question 4, looking back at the texts about the Mitfords to find the multi-word verbs used non-literally.

Answers

a. *He took up golf . . .*
b. *I came across an old school friend . . .*
c. *Jane and Andrew have broken up.*
d. *How do you get on with your parents?*
e. *She's always showing off about her wonderful children.*
f. *Are you beginning to settle down in your new flat?*
g. *. . . I gave it up.*
h. *Don't let me down.*
i. *She was told off . . .*
j. *. . . it didn't work out in practice.*

- Students work in pairs to complete the sentences.

Sample answers

a. *I've never been able to get on with Mary.*
b. *Did you come across him?*
c. *I think I'll take up jogging.*
d. *It's never once let me down.*
e. *He's always telling them off.*

● Listening

Aims

- fluency
- to develop students' listening abilities.

- Ask students if they know of countries where marriages are traditionally arranged by the parents of the couple, and have a brief discussion on the subject. You could ask questions such as the following.

Why are they arranged?
How are they arranged?
Would you like your marriage to be arranged?
Do you see any advantages in it?

- Read the introduction all together, then ask students to think of questions they would like answered from the interview.
  Ask them to read out their questions.

- Students listen to the interview and see if their questions are answered. Let them discuss in pairs.

- Play the tape again.
  Students work in pairs to answer the Comprehension Check questions.

Answers

1 He asked friends and relatives if they knew anyone, and found out about their education, background, and their family's background.
2 No.
3 The first man came in the morning and the second man in the evening. First her family spoke to them, then she was called in and she spoke to them for four or five minutes. Her father decided immediately.
4 To him, money was less important than education. He thought that if his daughter's husband was well-educated, he could earn money himself.
5 There was a special day when she went to visit Shyam's family and he came to visit her family, like an engagement party. They got married ten months later, and were often in touch, but if they met there was always a chaperon.

- Students work in pairs to correct the mistakes and complete the gaps.

Answers

Raj's father arranged her marriage *after she left school*, He chose her husband by *asking friends and relatives if they knew anyone suitable and finding out about their backgrounds.* In Raj's case, this didn't take long, but sometimes *a father can see up to a hundred men before he chooses one.* Two men were *interviewed by Raj's family, and her father decided that she should marry Shyam.* The men were of similar background, but one of them *was better educated although not so wealthy*, and this was the one *that her father chose. Raj agreed with her father, although she probably had little choice. She has now been married for twenty-two years, and in fact it has been a successful marriage. Most marriages in India are still arranged in this way, and the usual age for a girl to get married is sixteen or seventeen.*

- Do the 'What do you think?' questions all together. This should develop into a productive discussion. Questions 2 and 3 were designed to elicit some modal verbs of deduction.

Example

She must have felt very nervous.
Raj must come from an extremely wealthy family herself, if owning a village does not mean being wealthy.

Language focus

Aims

- accuracy
- to provide further controlled and freer practice of modal verbs of deduction.

- Do the Controlled Practice exercises 3 and 4.

As was suggested in the introduction to this unit, students tend to avoid using **might** and **could**, and express possibility by using **perhaps**. The aim of these two exercises is to provide further practice in expressing possibility. Exercise 3 is semi-controlled and exercise 4 is freer.

Do exercise 3 all together if you have a small class, or in groups if you have a large one.

Stress that it is not enough to say 'This is a Greek wedding' and stop. Unless students are *certain*, they must use a modal verb of deduction. They should also discuss the pictures at greater length, talking about the various people and objects.

Answers
The four wedding pictures are from Japan, India, Greece, and Britain.

- If you have access to two tape recorders, and ideally two rooms, your class could divide into two groups to do exercise 4 and work on one of the tapes only.

- Read the instructions all together. Play the two conversations. Students discuss their answers to the two questions in pairs.

Answers

In the first tape, a woman is being phoned by her ex-husband who wants to arrange to take their children out for the day. She complains that she hasn't had the money he is supposed to give her every month, and he tells her some good news about himself and presumably his new girlfriend – perhaps they're getting married.

In the second tape, a man receives a surprise phone-call from a very old friend. She asks him if she could stay with him for a few days while she is on a tour of Europe. He is a little embarrassed, because he is now a married man – they might have had an affair!

- Students choose one of the conversations and look at the tapescript, then work in pairs to reconstruct the other half of the conversation. Again, the aim is for students to use the modal verbs of deduction, so remind them of this, perhaps by putting some sample sentences on the board.

Example

It must be her ex-husband.
Here he might say something like 'Can I take the children out next Saturday?'

Sample answers
These sample answers serve only as a model, but naturally, there are many possibilities.

1 B. *Hello, it's Peter.*
   B. *Yes. How are you all?*
   B. *I want to make arrangements for taking the children out next Saturday. It's my turn.*
   B. *No, it's the twelfth, actually.*
   B. *I'm going to take them to the zoo.*

   B. *No, no, she really liked it, especially the lions and the monkeys.*
   B. *About ten, I thought.*
   B. *Actually, Barbara and I are getting married, so we've had quite a lot to buy.*
   B. *Thank you. I'll get a cheque to you as soon as I can, I promise.*
   B. *Bye.*

2 B. *Hello. Could I speak to Jeremy Brook, please?*
   B. *Oh, hi Jeremy. This is Janice Rosenberg.*
   B. *Janice Rosenberg. You remember me, don't you?*
   B. *Yes, you do. We met on holiday once.*
   B. *In 1983, in Greece.*
   B. *I'm fine. And yourself?*
   B. *Well, actually, I'm on another tour of Europe, and at the moment I'm in England, and at this moment I'm in Epsom.*
   B. *That's right. I was wondering if you could put me up for a few days.*
   B. *But you said I could always come to stay if I was in Epsom, don't you remember?*
   B. *Hey – are you married now?*
   B. *Well, that makes it kinda difficult, doesn't it. Well, don't worry, I won't bother you.*
   B. *No, I don't think that would be a good idea, do you?*
   B. *OK. Mind how you go, now. So long, Jeremy.*

● Vocabulary 2

Aims

- accuracy
- to help students find the correct entry and definition of an idiom.

- Learning idioms usually appeals to students, perhaps as a break from grammar, and perhaps because they perceive them as being 'the real language'. It is certainly useful to know how to find them in a dictionary and to recognize them in context, but it is questionable whether students should be over-encouraged to use them productively. Any mistake of grammar, word order, vocabulary, pronunciation, or stress can make the foreigner sound 'odd' to a native English speaker. Nevertheless, idioms are part of the language and the vocabulary system, and need gradually to be acquired.

- Read the introduction all together.
- Students work in pairs to do question 2, finding the idioms in their dictionary and paraphrasing them in non-idiomatic English.

● Speaking

Aims
- fluency
- to provide students with an opportunity for free speaking.

- The activity is similar in conception, aims and execution to the Maze in Unit 3. It is the kind of activity that is sometimes done on management training courses as it tests people's abilities to work co-operatively in groups, to organize themselves, and, above all, to know when to listen and when to speak. To a certain extent, it also 'sorts out the leaders from the led', because the way students approach it is entirely up to them. A dominant personality might successfully direct the class to the solution, or he/she might misinterpret and mislead, or might be so overpowering that the rest of the class refuse to co-operate! Similarly, a retiring personality might possess the vital piece of information, but if he/she doesn't volunteer it, the solution will never be reached!
- You will need to photocopy the cards on pages 56–7 of the Teacher's Book. You only need one copy, unless you have a very large class (over thirty), in which case students should work in two groups with two sets of cards.
- Read the introduction to the activity in the Student's Book. Having made sure all students understand what they have to do, tell them that *you are not going to help at all*. They

must decide how they are going to organize themselves, and must work together until they find the solution. Give out the fourteen cards. If you have fewer than fourteen students, give two cards out to some; if you have more than fourteen, some students can share. They are not playing a role, so the exact number of students doesn't matter.

- At this point you should sit down somewhere in the room where you are not the focus of attention, and prepare to take notes on the class's performance of the task (i.e. How did they organize themselves? Was everyone involved? Did everyone listen?); their linguistic performance (note especially grammatical, lexical and pronunciation mistakes), and the style of language the students chose to address each other in (too formal/informal/brusque?).

- What tends to happen at the start of this activity is that nobody does anything! Students might be so used to being directed by their teacher that they feel a little abandoned! If they ask you what they are supposed to do, *say nothing*! As long as your initial instructions were clear enough, you shouldn't need to step back in again. Slowly they will begin to organize themselves. What might happen is that one student suggests writing all the information up on the board, and another says

that this is a waste of time; another says 'Let's all read our cards out loud'. Soon it will dawn that the task entails matching names and professions to places in the room, and once this has been done, it is apparent who the murderer is.

- What sometimes happens is that students do in fact match names, professions and places in the room correctly, but then fail to realize that Brown must have been the murderer because no-one else moved and so no-one else could have put poison in his glass. If this happens, it is probably worth stepping in at this point to 'nudge' them to the solution. Frustration can have a negative effect on learning!

In the authors' experience, the record for solving the murder is about fifteen minutes; the average is about thirty-five.

- The roleplay was selected because it should involve a good deal of deducing, and hence lots of modals of deduction!
- When students have finished, ask them to discuss the questions in the Student's Book, which will help them to assess their performance of the task. You can then give your feedback from the notes you took while the activity was going on. If there were not many modal verbs of deduction, prompt students to create some at this point.

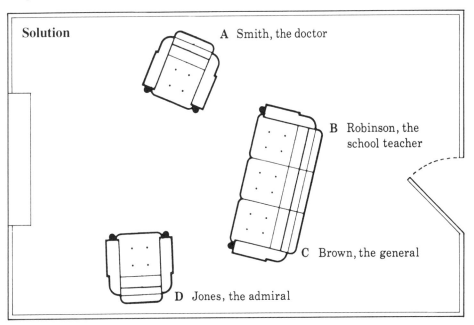

Solution

A Smith, the doctor

B Robinson, the school teacher

C Brown, the general

D Jones, the admiral

Information cards for the Murder Game

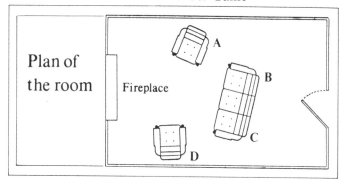

Plan of the room   Fireplace

A
B
C
D

Jones was drinking a whisky.

Four men are sitting in their club lounge.
In the room, there is a sofa and two
armchairs. Suddenly one of the men,
Jones, drops dead. His whisky has been
poisoned!

The school-teacher doesn't drink.

The school-teacher is sitting next to
Smith on his left.

The men's names are Jones, Smith, Brown
and Robinson.

Smith is sitting in one of the armchairs.

Robinson is sitting next to the general
on the sofa.

Their jobs are general, school-teacher,
admiral and doctor.

There are four people in the room.

© Oxford University Press Photocopiable

Smith is the admiral's brother-in-law.	Brown is drinking a beer.
No-one has left his chair.	Neither Smith nor Brown has any sisters.

● Writing

Aims

- accuracy
- to revise reported speech, and to highlight verb patterns which follow certain verbs that introduce reported speech.

- Do question 1 all together. The point is that when reporting, it is better to report the essential meaning, and not every word. Students may have got into the habit of word-for-word reporting from previous exercises that they have done on transforming direct to indirect speech.

Answers

Sentence 2 is better in both cases. The verbs **apologize** and **explain** identify the function of the utterance, and the sentences are succinct, leaving out unnecessary information.

- Students work in pairs to do question 2. They should look carefully at the verb patterns illustrated in the boxes. Stress the fact that the sentences must be *short*.

Answers

a. *He offered to give me a lift to the station.*
b. *Jeremy announced that he and Anita were getting engaged.*
c. *Peter's tutor suggested that he should start revising for his exam.*
d. *Johnny agreed that Annie's solution was best.*
e. *Beth complained that she had to do much more work than Philip.*
f. *James refused to lend his car to his son.*
g. *Stephanie explained why she couldn't go to the party.*
   or
   Stephanie explained that she couldn't go to the party because her son had the 'flu.
h. *She insisted that she had done her best to help.*

- The aim of question 3 is freer practice of reported speech. The best approach is probably to begin the exercise in class, so that you can be sure students know what they have to do, and then they finish it at home.

Play the tape once, and ask students to take notes. Let them compare their notes in pairs. Ask some questions to check comprehension.

Example

What is the crisis that the interviewer refers to?
Does the Prime Minister agree?
How does the Prime Minister justify the pay rise?
Is the Prime Minister going to get a pay rise?
Will it be more or less than the Members of Parliament?

The interview is intended to be humorous – try to get students to see this!

- Play the tape again, with students looking at the tapescript.

- Students begin to write in class. Allow at least ten or fifteen minutes for this, so that you have time to go round all the students, making sure they are reporting the essence of the interview, not every word.

REVISION

Aims

- accuracy
- to help students distinguish between some commonly confused words.

- These words are confused sometimes because they have similar meanings (for example, **remind** and **remember**), and sometimes because of interference from a students' first language. Such words are known as 'false friends', (for example, **controller** in French means to check; many Romance languages have a form similar to **actually** meaning **at the moment**).

- Students work in pairs to discuss the differences and to write sentences.

Answers

You **rob** a bank or a person; you **steal** money or a thing. **To rob** means 'to steal something from someone'.

Wait for suggests staying in the same place and doing nothing until something happens; for example, *waiting for a bus*. **Wait for** is more physical, while **expect** is more mental; if you expect something, you think it will probably happen whether you want it to or not; for example, *I'm expecting an important phone call/letter*. **Expect** can also mean 'to suppose'; for example, *I expect you're hungry after your walk*.

You **lend** something to somebody; you **borrow** something from somebody.

Lie is intransitive, that is, it cannot take an object, so you *lie in bed* or *lie on the beach*: **lay** is transitive, that is, it must have an object, so *to lay a table; A chicken lays eggs*.

To check means 'to examine' or 'to make sure'; for example, *to check the time of a train*, or *to check your homework*: **to control** means 'to direct or have power over'; for example, *The accelerator controls your speed*.

To fit means something is the right size; for example, *My shoes are uncomfortable because they don't fit me*: **to suit** means 'to match' or 'to look right with'; for example, *Green clothes suit her because she has ginger hair*. Whether something suits or not is subjective, whereas fit is objective.

To rise is intransitive; for example, *The sun rises and sets*: **to raise** is

transitive, for example, *to raise your hand, to raise a family*.

To remind means 'to make someone remember'; for example, *Remind me to leave a note for the milkman*.

Actually means 'in fact'; for example, *I know I look confident, but actually I'm very nervous*: **at the moment** means 'now'.

Loose is an adjective and means 'not fixed'; for example, *The leg of this chair is loose*: **to lose** is a verb.

You are **lucky** if you win a competition: **happy** means 'content', 'in a good mood'.

You **invent** something new; for example, *Bell invented the telephone*: you **discover** something that was always there; for example, *Columbus discovered America*.

Sensible means 'possessing common sense'; for example, *It is sensible to look both ways before crossing a road*: **sensitive** means 'easily offended', or 'aware of other people's feelings'. An example of the latter meaning is *Teachers must be sensitive to the problems of their students*.

A job is specific; for example, *He has a good job in a bank*: **work** is general; for example, *Digging the garden is hard work*. **Job** is countable, **work** is uncountable.

To take an exam means 'to do an exam'. If you do well, you **pass**; if you don't do well, you **fail**. (In French, *passer* means 'to take an exam').

UNIT 10

Expressing habit

Vice and virtue

AIMS OF THE UNIT

- The grammatical focus of this unit is expressing past and present habit. Students should be familiar with all the verb forms used, but the uses will probably be new. This is another example of the flexibility of the English language, where the same form can express several meanings.
- As **used to** + infinitive is one of the forms used for expressing past habit, it is contrasted with **be used to** + noun or gerund, meaning 'accustomed to'. This is a common confusion.
- Authentic listening practice is provided by the talk by Johnny Morris, a well-known writer and broadcaster.

NOTES ON THE LANGUAGE INPUT

Expressing past and present habit

The principal form used to express habit is, of course, the Present Simple. This unit introduces students to the Present Continuous to express an annoying habit, and unstressed **will** to express typical behaviour.

Examples

She's always asking me for money.
He'll spend hours just staring into space.

It is important not to confuse this unstressed use of **will** with the strong

stressed use which expresses insistence or strong volition.

Example

She 'will keep biting her nails.

This use expresses the attitude of the speaker (exasperation at someone else's obstinacy), which is not present in the unstressed use. It is not common, and the authors suggest that you do not draw students' attention to it.

To express past habit, English much prefers **used to** + infinitive to the Past Simple, and although students are often introduced to **used to** at an early stage in their learning, they may fail to use it on the occasions when it would sound best to an English ear.

Compare the following sentences:
When we were young, we went to the seaside for our holidays.
When we were young, we used to go to the seaside for our holidays.

To convey the same idea of habit, the first sentence needs the addition of *every year*.

Students can find it strange that this structure only exists to express past habit, not present, and may try to make it operate in the present.

Common mistakes

*Now I use to get up early, and I use to read the paper on the bus.

There is an element of confusion here with **be used to** (see below). **Used to** is one of the few verbs that can operate both as a modal verb and a full verb. The former of these is rare nowadays, and is not introduced in this unit.

Examples of **used to** as a modal verb:
I usen't to like cream, but now I love it.
Used you to play rugby at school?

'Be used to' + noun or gerund

Be used to and **used to (do)** are often confused. Their forms are very similar, and it is important to point out that in one form **used** is a verb whilst in the other it is an adjective.

Example

I used to wear short trousers.
used = a verb

I'm used to the cold weather.
used = an adjective.

The concepts are also confused because there is superficial similarity to do with habit, but in their fundamental concepts they are completely different. **Used to** + infinitive merely expresses a discontinued past habit. **Be used to** + noun or gerund expresses the idea of a difficulty encountered, an initial unpleasantness which has slowly been surmounted.

Students often express surprise that **to** can be followed by an **-ing** form, as in this structure. It should be pointed out that **used** is an adjective followed by a preposition, and as was seen in Unit 3, **-ing** forms follow all prepositions.

NOTES ON THE UNIT
 Discussion point

Aims

- fluency
- to launch the theme of the unit
- to introduce/revise some nouns and adjectives to describe character.

- As a lead-in, ask one or two students to describe the character of a friend of theirs, a boy/girl friend, or a parent, and the character of someone they don't like.
- Students look at the cartoon of Andy Capp, and in pairs discuss his vices.

Answers

He's lazy, he never works.
He doesn't pay any attention to his wife, and never listens to what she's saying.
He's unsympathetic to her problems and her pains.
He gambles.

- Students work in pairs to do question 2.

Answers

a.	positive	f.	negative
b.	negative	g.	negative
c.	negative	h.	negative
d.	negative	i.	positive
e.	positive	j.	negative

- Students work in pairs to do question 3.

Answers

f.	aggression	*aggressive*
b.	pride	*proud*
j.	obstinacy	*obstinate*
h.	meanness	*mean*
d.	greed	*greedy*
g.	jealousy	*jealous*
c.	deceit	*deceitful*
e.	sincerity	*sincere*
i.	reliability	*reliable*
a.	generosity	*generous*

- Discuss the two questions all together if you have a small class, or in groups if you have a large class. Let this go on for 5–10 minutes.

● Reading

Aims

- fluency
- to develop students' reading abilities
- to practise summarizing, by means of matching topic sentences to paragraphs.

- Read question 1 all together, and the possible titles. Explain that Scrooge is a character from a story by Charles Dickens. Scrooge was an extremely mean person, who refused to join in any celebrations because they cost too much money. His name has entered the English language.
Tell students to skim the article quickly, and set a time limit of thirty seconds.

Answer

c. is the best choice. It is not a statistical survey, so a. is wrong. The article criticizes these people, so b. is wrong. The article does not dwell on the fact that these people are all British; only one 'vice' is mentioned, not several; and the article has a humorous tone to it, which is not expressed by d.

- Read the introduction to question 2 all together.
Students work in groups of three to match the topic sentences to the correct paragraph. This is quite a demanding exercise, so allow adequate time for it, and encourage students who give in too easily.

Answers

a.	6	f.	10
b.	3	g.	7
c.	9	h.	8
d.	1	i.	2
e.	4	j.	5

- Students work in pairs to do the Comprehension Check/Language Work questions.

Answers

1 *Why did Paul Getty I have a pay-phone in his house?*
2 *Did he pay the ransom for the release of his grandson?*
3 *Why did a man buy his wife a card for belated birthday greetings?*
4 *Did he give it to her on her birthday?*
5 *Why does a woman ask for her birthday cards back?*
6 *Does the husband give his wife the vegetables he grows?*
7 *Why doesn't the woman have the central heating on during the day?*

- Answer the first 'What do you think?' question all together. Students work in pairs to devise dialogues in question 2. You could record some of the dialogues for intensive correction.

Language focus

Aims

- accuracy
- to practise expressions of frequency, and to provide students with controlled practice of the Present Continuous, **used to**, and **would** to express habit.

- Read the Language Review all together.
- Sentences for translation (see page iv of the Teacher's Book).

He always buys me flowers for my birthday.
She's always asking people for money.
We used to go to the seaside for our holidays, but we don't anymore.

- Students read the Grammar section in class.
- Do the Controlled Practice exercises 1–5.
Students work in pairs or small groups to answer them.

Answers

The answers for questions 1 and 3 are sample answers, as there are other possibilities.

1 a. *We go to the cinema twice a week.*
   b. *We eat out once or twice a year.*
   c. *He goes to church every Sunday morning.*
   d. *She plays tennis twice a month.*
   e. *She buys new clothes every week.*
   f. *I go to the dentist every six months.*
   g. *We have a bottle of wine with our supper every day.*
   h. *I have my hair cut once a month.*

2 There are no set answers for question 2.

3 a. *He's always forgetting where he's left things.*
   b. *He/she's always leaving the kitchen in a mess.*
   c. *She's always gossiping about people in the office.*

d. *He's always trying to kiss everyone.*
e. *He/she's always setting us homework and then forgetting to mark it.*

4 *liked*   b.   *got*   c.
   lived   b.   *had*   b.
   got up   a.   *climbed* a.
   crept   a.   *loved*   b.
   walked   c.   *went*   c.

5 First person   The past
                   Not very good

   Second person   The past
                   Good

   Third person   The present
                   Not very good

   Fourth person   The past
                   Good

- A discussion of the relationship students had with their parents could be fruitful at this point, with quite a lot of practice of past habits.

● Vocabulary 1

Aims

- accuracy
- to introduce students to a set of vocabulary relating to money.

- Discuss the two sayings all together, and encourage further discussion.
- Students work in pairs to divide the words in question 2 into categories.

Answers

borrowing money
a loan at 15% interest
a mortgage
a credit card
monthly repayments

Saving and investing money
a building society
to buy shares in a company
to earn 10% interest
the Stock Market
a piggy bank

personal bank account
to withdraw money
a current account
a cheque card
to cash a cheque
a monthly statement
a deposit account
to put money in

- Students work in pairs to do question 3.
  Well off and **hard up** are idiomatic expressions.
  Broke, quid, and **fiver** are slang.
- Students work in small groups to discuss question 4. The aim is to practise the vocabulary introduced in question 2, so be quite vigilant in your correction.

● Listening

Aims

- fluency
- to develop students' listening abilities
- to practise note-taking.

- Do the Pre-listening task all together. Let the discussion in questions 1 and 2 go on for as long as students are interested, and put students in pairs or small groups to do question 3, predicting the content of Johnny Morris's talk. Get some feedback on their predictions.
- Students listen to the talk and take notes. Just ask students to take a few notes, and not worry about detail. Johnny Morris is a very charismatic speaker, full of charm and humour, so encourage students to enjoy listening to him.
- Students compare notes with each other. Play the tape again for students to check. You could ask them to read the tapescript at the same time.
- Answer the 'What do you think?' questions all together. They should form the basis of a productive discussion. The English have a reputation for being animal lovers, but in our experience of using this material many other nationalities are the same!

Language focus

Aims

- accuracy
- to provide students with controlled practice of **be/get used to** + noun/gerund, and to contrast this with **used to** + infinitive.

- Read the Language Review all together.
- Sentences for translation (see page iv of the Teacher's Book).
  We used to go to the seaside, but we don't anymore.
  I'm used to getting up early in the morning.
  I'm used to the climate now, but at first I didn't like it.
  I'll never get used to the food.
- Do the Controlled Practice exercises 6 and 7.
  Students work in pairs.

  Some of the sentences in question 6 are a little banal, but the aim is to contrast starkly the difference between the two structures. Where short answers are possible, students also perceive that **used to** is a verb followed by a suppressed infinitive, *It used to (have)*, whereas **be used to** must be followed by a noun or a pronoun, *They're used to it.*

Answers

6 a. No set answer
  b. *They're used to it.*
  c. *It was difficult, but now I'm used to it.*
  d. *No, but she used to.*
  e. *No, but it used to.*
  f. *I suppose they're used to it.*
  g. No set answer
  h. *I suppose they get used to it.*

- Students work in pairs to write a short dialogue. The aim is freer practice of **be/get used to** + noun/gerund.
  When students have prepared their dialogues, ask them to read them out loud.

● Vocabulary 2

Aims

- accuracy
- to introduce students to collocation.

- One feature of the vocabulary system is that certain words go together, sometimes it seems for no reason other than that they do. This is called collocation. In some cases there may be a certain logic (for example, **to rent** is for a longer time than **to hire**), and at other times there is no logic (for example, why not **to do a phone call?**).

Collocation is seen in many combinations, for example, adjective + noun, verb + noun, verb + adverb or preposition, adjective + preposition. Preposition collocations are dealt with systematically in the Workbook.

- Students work in pairs to do question 1.

Answers
meanness
miserliness   tight-fisted habits
stinginess   penny-pinching
stories
tales
common
commonplace   widespread

- Read question 2 all together.

- Students do question 3 in pairs or small groups.

Encourage them to say the combinations out loud to see what 'sounds right'. This might appear to be rather a haphazard way of going about things, but often students can guess correctly what does or doesn't sound right, and this, of course, is invaluable to a language learner.

Answers
tall
person/tree/building
high
mountain/wall/price
heavy
traffic/smoker/rain
strong
drink/wind
loud
noise/music
to lose
your temper/a football match/ weight/your parents (they died)
to miss
a bus/a football match (on television)/*an opportunity/a TV programme/your parents*
Happy
New Year/Birthday/Christmas/ Anniversary
Merry
Christmas

to do
a lot of damage/your homework/ your best

to make
an appointment/sure/up your mind/a mess/an excuse/sense

● Speaking

Aims

- fluency
- to provide students with an opportunity for free speaking.

- Students divide into two groups to prepare their roles, looking at the suggestions in the Student's Book. Allow adequate time for this — ten minutes at least — as the group can not only help one another with ideas but should be able to make one another more accurate.

- Students pair up with a member of the other group to conduct the interview. Try to rearrange your room so that students are *facing* each other, with a table in between if possible, rather than next to each other in rows.

- The idea is that the writer should interview several candidates, and select one. If you have a small class, the writer could speak to all the candidates, but obviously this would not be possible with a larger class. You could set a time limit of five minutes for each interview, then clap your hands to signal 'Time to bring the interview to an end'. The interviewees must take their leave and move on to another interview. Do this perhaps three times, but don't let it go on until students' motivation flags.

- Answer question 4 all together. This is quite a light-hearted activity, and should produce some funny reasons for wanting or not wanting a particular companion.

● Writing

Aims

- accuracy
- to develop students' awareness of text cohesion.

- Rearranging jumbled texts involves a lot of reading and speaking, but the main aim is to point out to students how texts are organized, and how ideas are linked from sentence to sentence and paragraph to paragraph.

- Students work in groups of three to put the paragraphs in the correct order. This is quite a challenging exercise, so allow adequate time for it and encourage students who give up too easily.

Answers
Divorce   1 c.   2 d.   3 b.   4 h.
           5 a.   6 i.   7 m.   8 j.
Marriage   1 e.   2 g.   3 l.   4 o.
           5 f.   6 n.   7 k.

Students might argue that there are other possibilities, but they need to be checked carefully. Remember the way such newspaper articles are often organized — an eye-catching beginning, details of the people involved, the essence of the story, further details of the story, a memorable ending.

- Students write one of the essays from question 2. The aim of the first two is to revise ways of expressing present and past habit, and the aim of the third is to revise how to write a discursive essay.

REVISION
Aims

- accuracy
- to introduce or revise some lesser known but high-frequency time expressions.

- This is quite a straightforward area that students will probably have little difficulty in recognizing. Your aim is to encourage a high degree of accuracy in students' production of these items, especially their pronunciation.

- Students work in pairs to do question 1.

Answers
a. *Monday the 13th*
b. *Friday the 17th*

c. *Wednesday the 29th*
d. *Wednesday the 1st*
e. *Wednesday the 22nd*
f. *Saturday the 18th and Sunday
    the 19th*
g. *Friday the 24th*
h. *Wednesday the 8th*
i. *Thursday the 2nd*
j. *Thursday the 23rd*
k. *by Friday the 17th*

– It is essential that you now practise
  the time expressions in a.–k. with
  the real date. Students work in pairs
  to ask and answer the questions,
  writing down the answers. When
  they have finished, they ask and
  answer the questions across the
  class, and you can check whether
  they have the days and dates right,
  and whether their pronunciation is
  adequate. Look out for all aspects of
  pronunciation.

Example

Sentence stress

● • • • ●

Friday the thirteenth

● • ● •   ●

in a fortnight's time

Catenation

the eighth /ðɪ(j) eɪtθ/

Pronunciation of **the** before a vowel
sound:
the eighth /ðɪ / *not* /ðə/
the eleventh

Problem sounds
third /θ/
fourth

Consonant clusters
fifth /fθ/
sixth /ksθ/

– Students work in pairs to write
  sentences using the expressions in
  question 2.

UNIT 11

Hypothesis

It's easy to be wise after the event

AIMS OF THE UNIT

- This unit concentrates on hypothesizing about past events, and introduces **should/shouldn't have (done), wish** + various verb forms, and the third conditional. The first, second, and zero conditionals were introduced in *Headway Intermediate*. All conditionals are revised in the Workbook.
- The Reading section practises inferring a writer's intention, and inferring the meaning of words and expressions.
- The second Vocabulary section provides work on formal written language versus informal spoken language.

NOTES ON THE LANGUAGE INPUT

'Should' + perfect infinitive

This presents students with few problems of concept, apart from the need to select the simple or the continuous infinitive.

Example

You shouldn't have gone to the party. (complete action)

You should have been working. (activity over a period of time)

However, as with the third conditional, there are many contractions and weak forms in the pronunciation which students find difficult.

Example

/juː ʃʊdənt əv gɒn tə ðə pɑːtɪ /

'Wish'

The verb forms after wish are in fact subjunctive, an indicator of the unreality of the situation. As in the second conditional, this unreality is expressed by the verb form 'moving one tense back'. Once this has been pointed out, some students can operate the rules easily and accurately, while others fail to see the logic, so be prepared to deal with this.

Third conditional

Despite the apparent complexity of this structure, it presents students with no great problems of concept. Both main clause and condition clause are contrary to fact. However, no matter how often students have done work on this structure, they encounter tremendous problems of form and pronunciation. There are so many 'bits' for them to get right; for example, **if** + Past Perfect; using **had/hadn't**; Past Perfect Simple or Continuous; **would** + perfect infinitive; remembering to include **have**, and to get the past participle correct. Given the above, it is no wonder that pronunciation suffers.

The best you can do is give students a lot of controlled practice in forming and pronouncing the structure, and be vigilant in your correction of it in normal classroom interaction.

NOTES ON THE UNIT
 Discussion point

Aims

- fluency
- to test students' abilities at recognizing and producing **should/shouldn't have (done)** and the third conditional.

- A lead-in to this activity is to have a brief discussion about a time in the students' lives when something went wrong. You could reply to their tales using the target structures, or prompting them to use them.

- Read the introduction to question 1 all together, then students read the five stories. Smiles and laughter will indicate comprehension. Conduct the discussion about what the criminals should or shouldn't have done — all together if you have a small class, or otherwise in groups.

- Students work in groups to answer question 2. Notice that the last question prompts them to use the main clause only of the third conditional.

Example

I wouldn't have done that. I'd have run away.

- You could extend this discussion by asking students about times in their lives when they had been faced with danger, and what they did. Take care not to offend, however, as students might have extremely unhappy recollections of the event.

Reading

Aims
- fluency
- to develop students' reading abilities
- to practise inferring a writer's intention, and inferring the meaning of words and expressions.

- 'Reading between the lines' is something that native speakers do all the time, and this means both you and your students. We unconsciously fill in the gaps, relate one point of a story to another, infer a writer's attitude to what he/she is saying and understand as much from what *isn't* said as what is. These skills naturally need practising in a foreign language.

- Students work in groups to do the Pre-reading task. Don't let this go on too long — about five minutes is enough. Get some feedback from the groups.

- Read the introduction to the text all together, check their understanding of the colloquial language, and read the introduction to Jack Higgins. Remind students of the pre-reading task, and ask them if they think Jack Higgins is/was all those people. Talk about this for a minute, then tell students that he is/was. Ask them briefly to predict what they think his regrets might be.

- Students read the text, answering the two questions. Allow students adequate time to read — about five minutes. Draw their attention to the glossary to help with some background information or difficult words. When they are ready, ask them to discuss their answers to the two questions in pairs.

Answers
1 15 No, because people thought he was stupid.
  18 No, because he didn't have an older person to go to for advice; because when he was a teenager, it was a handicap to be young; because he listened to other people's opinions too much; because he didn't have any qualifications; because a friend of his was shot dead while he was doing his military service.
  31 Probably. He got his degree, which he said he longed for, but he also says it didn't mean much.
  42 Yes, because this was his first real break.
2 Probably not. He says life has been a disappointment; he has achieved all his ambitions; there is nothing he really wants to do; his life is empty.

- Students work in groups of three to answer the Comprehension Check questions.

Answers
1 This is quite a difficult question. Draw students' attention to the date on the article. In 1982 he was 53. Therefore he was born in 1929; and in 1971, when he had his first success as an author, he was 42. It is probably a good idea to tell students this at the outset. In the answers, a question mark next to an event means that we do not know for sure exactly when it happened, but we can use logic to guess.
  1 *lived in Belfast.*
  2 *did National Service.*
  3 (?) *did several clerical jobs.* (We presume this was after his National Service.)
  4 (?) *acted in Leeds.* (His friends at the time were office workers, so it must have been around the same time as 3.)
  5 *got a degree.*
  6 (?) *was a tutor at university.* (This happened some time after getting his degree and working as a lecturer. He 'finally' became a tutor, when he was perhaps 37 or 38.)
  7 (?) *started writing.* (The introduction at the top of the article tells us he was a tutor before being successful as a writer. Perhaps he started writing while he was a tutor.)
  8 (?) *wrote* The Eagle has Landed.
  9 (?) *became a millionaire.*

2 **Sample answers**
  He wishes he had known an older person that he could have talked to.
  He wishes he had been more confident.
  He wishes he hadn't worked in offices, wasting his energies.
  He wishes he had started writing earlier.
  He wishes he had acted.

- Students work in groups to answer the 'What do you think?' questions. These might take a while to do thoroughly, and you could choose either to spread the remaining exercises on the text over two lessons, or set some for homework, for example, 1 and 3.

Answers
1 Line 14
  He was a teenager from 1942 to 1948, at a time when there was no teenage culture or tradition, and teenagers were kept in their place because they were young and inexperienced.

  Line 48
  People told him that his ideas for books were terrible, but he went ahead and wrote them anyway, and they were successful.

  Line 66
  Presumably, it sold more copies more quickly than any book published previously.

  Line 80
  He seems to be showing off a little, saying that he was able to appreciate grand works of literature when he was 'a lad', without any instruction or anyone telling him what he should read.

  Line 88
  It wasn't that important to him. (Or at least, that is what he says now. One suspects he was quite pleased at the time.)

  Line 111
  This seems to express his fundamental cynicism, as though he basically expects life to be disappointing. One gets the impression that he is rather selfish.

Line 117
He has achieved all the ambitions he set himself.

Line 132
This could mean several things. Perhaps he feels that he, Jack Higgins, should not be mixing with such people; that success should not open the doors to such illustrious people; or perhaps that these people should not want to talk to him as a person, but simply because he is a millionaire.

Line 134
Again, this is an example of his cynicism. He doesn't think that there is much point or purpose in anything. For him, the following proverb is apt: 'It is better to travel hopefully than to arrive'.

2 There is no set answer here. Students might argue for or against the various adjectives, but make sure they justify their answers.

In the opinion of the authors, the following adjectives describe him:

self-confident, although he wasn't when he was younger
hard-working, because he calls himself a workaholic
wise, no, although he thinks he is (see paragraph 1)
proud of his writing achievements and his ability to improve himself
home-loving, because he seems to appreciate his wife and children
disillusioned, because he doesn't see the worth of his achievements
self-made, because he came from a poor background
cynical, because of his attitude to life

3 a persistent idea = *obsession*
a disadvantage = *a handicap*
worked hard at and was successful in = *got to grips with*
had the courage = *had the guts* (slang)
wanted very much = *longed*
lucky opportunity = *break*
shocked, troubled = *shaken*
obsessed by, addicted to = *hooked*

a person who does not finish a course of study = *drop-out*
chances of professional advancement = *career prospects*

Language focus

Aims
- accuracy
- to provide students with controlled practice of **wish** + appropriate verb form and **should** + perfect infinitive.

- Read the Language Review all together.
- Sentences for translation (see page iv of the Teacher's Book).

  You shouldn't have gone to the party.
  You should have been working for your exams.
  I wish I wasn't fat.
  I wish I had more friends.
  I wish I had worked harder at school.
  I wish I could swim.
  I wish you would help me.

- Students read the Grammar section in class.
- Do the Controlled Practice exercises 1–3. Students work in pairs.

Answers

1 a. *I wish my parents hadn't made me get a safe job.*
   b. *I wish I had tried to become a professional actor.*
   c. *I wish I had been encouraged to be a writer.*
   d. *I wish I hadn't had to do National Service.*
   e. *I wish I wasn't a workaholic.*
   f. *I wish I didn't find life disappointing.*
   g. *I wish I had some hobbies.*
   h. *I wish I could be a member of Mensa.*

2 **Sample answers**
   a. *I wish I didn't have a hangover. I shouldn't have had so much to drink last night.*
   b. *I wish I hadn't crashed the car. I should have come home by taxi.*

   c. *I wish I didn't have to go to court. I should have remembered to pay the parking fine.*
   d. *I wish my wife hadn't left me. I should have treated her more fairly.*
   e. *I wish I wasn't late for work. I should have got up when the alarm went off.*

- Students work in pairs to write dialogues in question 3. When they are ready, ask some of them to read their dialogues out loud.

● Speaking

Aims
- fluency
- to provide students with an opportunity for free speaking.

- The time taken up by this discussion depends on your timetable and the interests of your students. They might want to discuss questions 2 and 3 at length, or merely give one-line answers.

Answers

In the opinion of the authors, all the paradoxes in question 3 are possible. This is the question in the Speaking section that could last the longest, by encouraging discussion and exemplification of each paradox.

● Vocabulary 1

Aims
- accuracy
- to introduce students to a set of vocabulary related to driving.

- As a lead-in, you could ask students if they have a car, if they like driving, how much they drive, and so on.
- Students work in pairs to do question 1.

Apart from practising various vocabulary items to do with cars, this question also practises many multi-word verbs and prepositions.

Examples

to get in
to put your belt on
to put the key in the ignition
to put your foot on the accelerator
to look in the mirror
to look behind you
to put the indicator on
to go into first gear
to let the handbrake off

- Monitor the pairs carefully, stepping in to correct and feed in new words.

- Students form new pairs, one reading out instructions whilst the other mimes.

- Do question 3 all together.

Answers

breaking the speed limit
going through red lights
cutting a corner
overtaking on the inside lane
parking on a zebra crossing
parking on the pavement
double parking
people not wearing seat belts

- Students answer question 4 in pairs, using dictionaries.

Answers

On *a dual carriageway*, the two sides of the road are separated by a barrier. You can't stop on a dual carriageway. There are usually two lanes on each side of the road.

In *a one-way street*, traffic moves in one direction only. You can't reverse in them.

A cul-de-sac is a road with one opening only. Notice the pronunciation.

A by-pass is a road which goes around a town or village, so that traffic avoids populated areas.

A flyover is a road or bridge which goes over another road.

- Do question 5 all together.

Answers

You *dip your lights* when driving at night so as not to dazzle drivers coming in the opposite direction. You *flash your lights* to signal to another driver, either to say 'I'm coming' or 'Come on'.

You *do a U-turn* if you want to travel in the opposite direction. You must make sure that the road is clear.
You *sound your horn* to signal to another driver or a pedestrian.
You *swerve* to avoid hitting something.
You *slam on your brakes* in order to stop quickly.

● Listening

Aims

- fluency
- to develop students' listening abilities.

- Although driving and taking driving tests is hardly the most controversial subject, it is one which often interests students as most adults these days learn to drive.

- Students do the Pre-listening task all together if it is a small class, or otherwise in groups. Let this go on for as long as students are interested.

- Read the introduction to the tape very carefully, making sure that students understand what they have to do while they are listening. They need to both put a cross in the box of the relevant sections, and underline the relevant phrases.

- Let students read through the Statement of Failure. You should sort out any problems of vocabulary.

- Play the tape. It is quite amusing, so encourage your students to enjoy it.

- Students check their answers in pairs. Play the tape again for them to check.

- Answer the 'What do you think?' questions all together.

Answers

Department of Transport Road Traffic Act 1972   Test Centre: _____

Statement of Failure to Pass Test of Competence to Drive

Name _____

has this day been examined and has failed to pass the test of competence to drive prescribed for the purposes of section 85 of the Road Traffic Act 1972.

Date _____

_____
Authorised by the Minister of Transport to conduct tests

Examiners have regard to the items listed below in deciding whether a candidate is competent to drive. The matters needing special attention are marked for your information and assistance and should be studied in detail.

1. ✖ Comply with the requirements of the eyesight test.
2. ☐ Know the Highway Code.
3. ☐ Take proper precautions before starting the engine.
4. ✖ Make proper use of/accelerator/clutch/gears/footbrake/handbrake/steering.
5. ✖ Move away/safely/under control.
6. ✖ Stop the vehicle in an emergency/promptly/under control/making proper use of front brake.
7. ✖ Reverse into a limited opening either to the right or left/under control/with due regard for other road users.
8. ☐ Turn round by means of forward and reverse gears/under control/with due regard for other road users.
9. ☐ Make effective use of mirror(s) and take effective rear observation well before signalling/changing direction/slowing down or stopping.
10. ☐ Give signals/where necessary/correctly/in good time.
11. ☐ Take prompt and appropriate action on all/traffic signs/road markings/traffic lights/signals given by traffic controllers/other road users.
12. ☐ Exercise proper care in the use of speed.
13. ☐ Make progress by/driving at a speed appropriate to the road and traffic conditions/avoiding undue hesitancy.
14. ✖ Act properly at road junctions: –
    – regulate speed correctly on approach;
    – take effective observation before emerging;
    – position the vehicle correctly/before turning right/before turning left;
    – avoid cutting right-hand corners.
15. ☐ Overtake/meet/cross the path of/other vehicles safely.
16. ☐ Position the vehicle correctly during normal driving.
17. ✖ Allow adequate clearance to stationary vehicles.
18. ☐ Take appropriate action at pedestrian crossings.
19. ☐ Select a safe position for normal stops.
20. ✖ Show awareness and anticipation of the actions of/pedestrians/cyclists/drivers.

Language focus

Aims

- accuracy
- to provide students with controlled practice of the third conditional.

- Read the Language Review all together.
- Sentences for translation (see page iv of the Teacher's Book).
  If I had worked hard, I would have passed the exam.
  If she had driven more carefully, she might have passed the test.
  If I had been watching the road, I wouldn't have hit the tree.
- Students read the Grammar section in class.
- Do the Controlled Practice exercises 4–7.
  Students work in pairs or small groups to do exercises 4 and 5.

Answers

4 a. *If she had been more confident, she would have passed.*
  b. *If she hadn't been nervous, she would have remembered to let the handbrake off.*
  c. *She wouldn't have skidded if she hadn't lost control.*
  d. *If she had known the names of cars, she could have read the number-plate.*
  e. *The examiner wouldn't have put the brakes on if she had been paying more attention.*

5 **Sample answers**
  a. *If he hadn't gone to Dallas, he wouldn't have been assassinated.*
  b. *If I had been staying in that hotel, I might have been killed.*
  c. *If I hadn't gone to the party, I wouldn't have met my wife.*
  d. *I wouldn't have lost the match if I had concentrated more.*
  e. *If she had been on the hijacked aircraft, she might have been injured.*

- Do exercise 6 all together. The aim is to practise just the main clause of the third conditional, as this is often how they are used. The condition is

understood, and is not repeated as each person adds their own opinion.
There are no set answers, but insist on good pronunciation, with attention to contractions and weak forms.

- Ask students to read through the dialogue with gaps in exercise 7. Make sure there are no problems of vocabulary.
  Play the tape once only, and put students in pairs to reconstruct the gaps. The aim should not be memory, nor a dictation, but controlled practice of the target structures of the unit.
  Allow adequate time for this – about ten minutes, then play the tape again for students to check. They could consult the tapescript as a final check.

● Vocabulary 2

Aims

- accuracy
- to help students to become aware of the differences between formal written English and informal spoken English.

- Style is an area of the language where students' receptive abilities will nearly always exceed their productive abilities. For the most part, students use a neutral, perhaps rather informal, style in both their speaking and their writing, and it is an exceptionally high-level student who can switch between, or select, different styles. Remember, however, that non-linguistic features such as gesture as much as the selection of certain language items make an utterance more or less polite, or more or less formal.
- Students do the questions in pairs.

Answers

1 a. 9 *Make use of mirrors before changing direction.*
  b. 9 *Take rear observation.*
  c. 12 *Exercise proper care in the use of speed.*
  d. 14 *Regulate speed correctly on approaching a road junction.*

  e. 14 *Take observation before emerging.*
  f. 17 *Allow adequate clearance to stationary vehicles.*
  g. 20 *Show awareness and anticipation of the actions of pedestrians, etc.*

2 a. In a restaurant.
  Please don't smoke here.
  b. On a train or bus.
  Please give up this seat if an old or infirm person needs it.
  c. On a food packet.
  If you don't like them or there's something wrong with them, send them back and tell us when and where you bought them, and we'll give you your money back.
  d. On the wall of any public building.
  If there's a fire, get out quick!
  e. A letter from a bank manager.
  In a recent letter, I told you that you've overdrawn your account by over £500, and I asked you not to cash any more cheques, and you said that you were going to pay off the overdraft. So I was really surprised when I found out that you'd been using your cash card. You haven't got any money in your account! Please don't use your cash card again, and don't write any cheques until you've paid off your overdraft and you've put some money into your account.

- Students work in pairs to enact the interview between the bank manager and the customer. It should revise some of the vocabulary introduced in Unit 10.

● Writing

Aims

- accuracy
- to practise sentence combination, producing complex sentences and coherent paragraphs.

- As a lead-in, put the following sentences on the board, and ask students to join them to make one sentence.

Joan Colby is an actress.
She lives in Hollywood.
She recently divorced her fifth husband.
She is going to learn Russian.
She has been offered a part in a new production of War and Peace.

Answer

Joan Colby, the Hollywood actress who recently divorced her fifth husband, is going to learn Russian because she has been offered a part in a new production of War and Peace.

– Discuss the ways in which the sentences were combined.
– Students read the sentences about Hemingway.
– Ask students to say where they think paragraphs might begin and end.
– Students begin to combine the sentences in class, and finish it for homework.

Sample answer

Ernest Hemingway was born in Illinois, a suburb of Chicago, in 1899. He had a middle-class upbringing, and his father was a doctor, but all his life he rebelled against the morals of his parents and the conventions of life in Chicago.

He graduated from High School in 1917, but, being impatient for a less sheltered environment, he didn't go to college. Instead, he went to Kansas City, where he was employed as a reporter for a leading newspaper, the Star, *and this gave him invaluable vocational training.*

He wanted to be a soldier, but was rejected for military service because he had poor eyesight, so he became an ambulance driver for the American Red Cross. He was injured in World War I, and also decorated for heroism.

He was fascinated by war, working as a war correspondent in Spain, China, and Europe, and many of his books were about war. For Whom the Bell Tolls, *his most successful book, was written in 1940, and is about a volunteer American soldier in the Spanish Civil War. This book*

dealt with the comradeship of war, whereas A Farewell to Arms *is about the pointlessness of war.*

He won the Nobel prize for literature in 1954, but he suffered from depression towards the end of his life. He loved life, but he was obsessed with death, and he committed suicide in 1961.

REVISION

Aims

– accuracy
– to practise identifying main sentence stress
– to practise contrastive stress and wide voice range.

– Broadly speaking, it is true to say that students' intonation, voice range, and sentence stress are better in real situations (which probably means outside the classroom) than in unstimulating, simulated ones. Sentence stress, and shifting stress to show contrast, is a feature of many other languages, but all the same it *does* need pointing out and practising.
– Students work in pairs to mark where the main sentence stress is in question 1.

Answers

a. *I thought you'd given it to him.*

b. *I thought you'd given it to him.*

c. *I thought she was French.*

d. *I thought of it first.*

e. *No, he works for me.*

f. *He works for me.*

g. *The chips were nice.*

– It is now essential that the two-line dialogues are practised thoroughly, both in open pairs so you can monitor, and in closed pairs. You will have to exaggerate in your own models to ensure an adequate voice range from your students.
– Read through the introduction to question 2 all together, then students answer the questions in pairs.
– Read through the introduction to question 3 all together, and drill the sample corrections.

Play the tape. As soon as students think they hear a mistake, they must tell you to stop the tape. Again, when they correct the mistakes, insist on accurate intonation and wide voice range.

Answers

*He doesn't live in **New York**. He lives in **Jersey**.*
*He hasn't got **six** children. He's only got **four**.*
*He wasn't born in **London**. He was born in **Belfast**.*
*He isn't **forty** three. He's **fifty** three.* (Unless students want to work out his exact age now!)
*He **did** leave school at fifteen.*
*He didn't go to **Australia**. He went to **Berlin**.*
*He **doesn't** have a happy life. He finds life disappointing.*
*He **doesn't** enjoy meeting the Royal Family.*

– Students work in pairs to devise some sentences about their colleagues that are factually wrong. Give some examples, so students know what you want.

Example

*Jean **isn't** married.*
*Maria **hasn't** got a car.*
*Pedro **doesn't** like football.*

Students read out their sentences for the others to correct.

UNIT 12

Articles

Time

AIMS OF THE UNIT

- This unit aims to lay a foundation for the learning of articles in English, an area which always causes problems.
- There is a theme of time, which is exploited in the reading and in the listening. The latter takes the form of an authentic interview with Margaret Thatcher, the first woman Prime Minister in Britain. There is also a poem by E. Nesbit on the subject of life and death.
- In the first Vocabulary section there is an exercise on multi-word verbs, and an introduction to nouns formed from multi-word verbs.

Almost any topic could have been chosen as a vehicle to practise articles, because they pervade the language. The topics of time, life and death, and morality were chosen because they require students to speak in generalities (for example, *Life is so short*; *Independence is an important quality*, and this is an area where students often introduce articles incorrectly, making statements such as *The life is short*.

This unit, as with all the others in *Headway Upper-Intermediate*, has both accuracy-based and fluency-based activities. In theory, your attention to errors should be greater in the former, but there is a case for correcting mistakes in the target language even during fluency-based work if it can be done without interrupting the flow of the activity too much.

silently at their own pace because the quiz contains some quite difficult items, and you would end up explaining the same item again and again as different students encountered it.

- Ask a student to read out loud the question and the multiple choice answers, sorting out any problems and discussing the question as necessary.
- Students add up their scores, and read the relevant interpretation. Let them do this first on their own as their motivation to see if they agree should be quite high.
- Ask if they agree, then have a student read out loud the interpretations, with you checking comprehension and vocabulary. Encourage discussion at this point.

NOTES ON THE LANGUAGE INPUT

Articles

It could well be argued that the use of articles in English is unteachable. They are used in a similar way in many other European languages, but in English there are many exceptions to the rules. Speakers of those languages where there are no articles (for example, Arabic and Japanese) encounter problems of all sorts, frequently omitting articles altogether. The aim of this unit is to present the basic rules so that students can begin to perceive the logic that is present.

NOTES ON THE UNIT

● Discussion point

Aims
- fluency
- to launch the theme of time, and to prepare students for the reading text that follows.

- As a lead-in, ask students questions such as the following:
  Do you use your time productively?
  Are you always busy, or always lazy?
  What do you do with your free time?
- Do the quiz all together. This is preferable to students reading

 Reading

Aims
- fluency
- to develop students' reading abilities
- to practise predicting content and summarizing.

- Students do the Pre-reading task in pairs. When they have discussed the graffiti, get some feedback, asking students which they like best, which is most true, etc. Ask them which are humorous and which aren't, but be prepared for students to have differing views on this!
- Ask students to read the headline only, and explain that this article appeared in the *London Evening*

70

Standard, a popular evening newspaper, so if the article deals with a vaguely philosophical topic, it will be 'popular' philosophy, not academic.

- Students read the first two paragraphs. There are some difficult vocabulary items which you could explain quickly if they cause great problems, but otewise don't bother.
- Students work in groups of three to discuss the ideas and topics they expect the article to mention. Allow at least five minutes for this. Get the feedback, asking students to justify their opinions. This should develop into a class discussion, as students support or refute why certain topics will or will not appear in the article.
- Students read the rest of the article, discussing the true/false questions in pairs.

Answers

1 True
2 False
3 True
4 False
5 True
6 False
7 True – richer in quality, not materialistically.
8 False
9 True

- Discuss the 'What do you think?' questions all together. There are no set answers.

Sample answers

1 Cinderella waiting for a fairy godmother.
  Something between b. and d.
2 They both valued the quality of their lives above their materialistic wealth; they both knew what they enjoyed doing, and arranged their lives so that they could do it.
3 *Real Life* with capital letters is what we say will begin when such-and-such a hurdle has been got over, but in fact *real life* with small letters is now, and the only life we have.

- Students mark the text on their own, then compare in pairs.
  Sort out any points that students don't understand.

- Discuss questions 5 and 6 all together. This could develop into a productive discussion.
- Students could do the summary either in class or for homework.

Language focus

Aims

- accuracy
- to give students controlled practice in the use of **a**, **the** and the zero article.

- Read the Language Review all together.
- Sentences for translation (see page iv of the Teacher's Book).

I bought a jumper and a tie.
She's a doctor.
What a nice day!
I bought the jumper for Alice, and the tie is for me.
I went to the cinema last night.
Dogs make very good pets.
Love is eternal.

- Do the Controlled Practice exercises 1–5.
  Students work in pairs to do questions 1–3.

Answers

1 a. *an interesting chap, a party* – indefinite article because they are mentioned for the first time.
  b. *in bed, at school* – no article, because they are common prepositional phrases.
  c. *life, surprises* – no article, because it is a general statement.
  d. *the life of Mozart* – definite article because the noun is defined.
  e. *The Amazon, the longest river, the world* – definite article because they are unique.
  f. *a month* – indefinite article in a numerical expression.
  g. *the bank* – definite article because it is a public place, and *which* bank is either understood or doesn't matter.
  h. *the flowers* – definite article because the listener and speaker both know which flowers are being referred to.

  i. *Birds, winter* – no article, because it is a general statement.

2 a. *for breakfast*
  b. no mistakes
  c. *the United States*
  d. no mistakes
  e. *a very good programme*
  f. *to school*
  g. *a small house*
  h. *Italian food*
  i. no mistakes

3 a. *to prison for the murder*
  b. *at work   in hospital*
     an operation   The doctor
  c. *The lunch*
     We had soup with garlic bread
     a lovely Mexican dish with rice
     the most delicious ice-cream
  d. *a degree in modern languages.*
     I studied French language and literature at Bristol University.
  e. *the actress   in Oxford Street*
     an Oscar
     The Taming of the Shrew
  f. *Beauty is in the eye of the beholder.*
  g. *Cats are interesting creatures.*
     the day   at night
  h. *the lights   the doors*
     wasting energy
     the electricity bill

- You might choose to play 'Just a minute' in another lesson.

  The aim is light-hearted but intensive practice of articles. Students are invited to talk about any of the subjects, and usually they begin by talking generally, so no articles are used. They can then go on to talk about any aspect of the subject, which might involve any of the uses of articles.

  Have a run-through of the game first, so students see what they have to do, then begin in earnest! Students are usually hesitant at first to interrupt and correct, so encourage this to happen, perhaps by stopping the speaker yourself. Ideally, you will need a stop-watch. Many watches these days have this facility.

- Students work in pairs to discuss question 5.

Answers

a. *the key* — we know which one.
   a key — it could be any key.
b. *Few people* — not many. The
   idea is negative.
   A few people — a certain
   number. The idea is positive.
c. *in prison* — the suggestion is that
   he committed a crime and has
   been sentenced to go to prison.
   in the prison — the suggestion is
   that he is visiting someone in
   prison, probably a prisoner.
d. *Mr Smith* — we both know
   which one.
   A Mr Smith — a certain
   gentleman, we don't know who
   he is.
e. *in a caravan* — merely gives
   information.
   in one caravan — expresses
   surprise that so many people
   could go on holiday in just one
   caravan.

● Vocabulary 1
Aims

- accuracy
- to introduce students to more
  examples of multi-word verbs, and
  to show how they can sometimes be
  used as nouns.

- Students work together in pairs to
  do question 1.

Answers

a. *broke down*
b. *came back*
c. *taken over*
d. *took away*
e. *took off*
f. *cutting back*
g. *building up*
h. *held up*

- Read the introduction to nouns
  formed from multi-word verbs all
  together. Students work in pairs to
  do exercise 2. This might seem
  straightforward, but it can present
  students with difficulties as they are
  being introduced to a part of the
  vocabulary system that they are
  probably unfamiliar with, so allow

adequate time, and be prepared to
help and encourage.

Answers

a. *take-off*
b. *come-back*
c. *take-away*
d. *breakdown*
e. *Cutbacks* or *cut-backs*
f. *hold-up*
g. *take-overs*
h. *build-up*

- There is a further exercise on this
  area in the Workbook.

● Speaking
Aims

- fluency
- to provide students with an
  opportunity for free speaking.

- Students work in groups of four to
  put the events and eras in the
  correct place on the diagram. Not
  everyone's knowledge of world
  events is wide, so be prepared for
  some wild guesses!

Answers

3000 BC   *Egyptian Empire*
2000 BC   *Ancient Chinese
   civilisation*
500BC–476 AD   *Roman Empire*
0   *Birth of Jesus Christ*
570   *Birth of Muhammad*
1492   *Discovery of America*
16th century   *Colonization of South
   America*
18th century–1945   *British Empire*
18th and 19th century   *Colonization
   of Africa*
1804–1815   *Napoleonic era*
1917   *Russian revolution*

You could extend the discussion by
asking students what they know
about these events and eras.

- Discuss question 2 in groups if you
  have a large class, or all together if
  you have a smaller class. It is
  usually of great interest to everyone
  to hear what individuals have to say.
- Students work first alone to answer
  question 3. Students should then
  compare their lists, discussing the

extent to which the objects typify
this period in world history.

● Listening
Aims

- fluency
- to develop students' listening
  abilities.

- This is an authentic interview, and
  whatever students' political views,
  or indeed their interest in politics
  generally, they usually feel a great
  sense of achievement if they can
  understand a famous person talking.
- Students divide into two groups to
  do the Pre-listening task. Allow
  adequate time for this, as it will
  provide preparation for the actual
  interview. A spokesperson for each
  group reads out their facts and
  opinions.
- Play the interview. Encourage
  students to 'sit back and enjoy it',
  rather than worry about unknown
  words.
- Students work in pairs to answer the
  Comprehension Check questions.
  Play the tape again for them to
  check, possibly reading the
  tapescript at the same time.

Answers

1 *Hard work, self-reliance, living
   within your income, cleanliness
   being next to godliness, self-
   respect, helping neighbours, pride
   in your country, a sense of duty.*
2 *The existence of workhouses, bad
   conditions in factories.*
3 *If people did well in Victorian
   times, they then helped others less
   fortunate. Private prosperity led
   to people voluntarily helping others,
   building hospitals and schools.*
4 *It gives you an interest in the
   future, respect for your own
   property, and something to hand
   on to your children and
   grandchildren. It enables people
   to be independent.*
5 *They cannot have the freedom of
   choice to buy their own house, to*

pay for their children's education, and to pay for private health care.

- Discuss the 'What do you think?' questions all together.

● Writing

Aims

- accuracy
- to practise linking devices of ordering (**first, next, finally**) and to compare them with potentially confusing items (**at first, at last**)
- to practise various markers of opinion (**actually, fortunately, naturally**).

- Students have great problems using **actually**, confusing it with **at the moment**. Also, they often try to use **after** as an adverb, not realizing that it is only a preposition. This leads to mistakes such as *We went out for a meal. After, we came home.*
- Students work in pairs to put the correct linking device into each gap.

Answers

a *Naturally*
b *still*
c *At first*
d *While*
e *First*
f *Next*
g *until*
h *Meanwhile*
i *finally*
j *Fortunately*
k *Afterwards*
l *Actually*

- Students write an essay about a time in their lives that is important to them. They might well need to use some of the linking devises practised in question 1.

● Vocabulary 2

Aims

- accuracy
- to practise working out the meaning of an unknown word from the context of a dictionary definition
- to read and appreciate a poem.

- Read the introduction to question 1 all together.
  Students work in pairs to try to work out the meaning from the example sentence, then check in a dictionary for the definition.
- Students work in pairs to divide the words in question 2 into three categories.

Answers

health
sores, pains, a cure, a herb, sprains

food
a hare, a herb, a trout, greens, to baste

household chores
to sweep, to sew, to dust

- Students listen to the recording of the poem and read it at the same time.

  There are many ways to approach a poem in class. The authors think that students like to feel quite sure that they have understood nearly every word before discussing it. After all, reading a poem is not like reading a newspaper article, where understanding despite the presence of unknown words is an important skill. After students have heard the poem once, read it again yourself, pausing whenever necessary to check comprehension and ensure that words and ideas are understood.

- Students do question 1 in pairs. They might argue that there is no single best choice, but in the opinion of the authors d. is best. (See the first line of the last verse.)
- Students work in pairs to answer question 2.
- Answer the remaining questions all together. Depending on your class's interests, a fruitful discussion should ensue. Notice that E. Nesbit was writing at the beginning of the century, and there have probably been more changes in the world in this generation than at any other time in world history.

REVISION

Aims

- accuracy
- to practise certain nouns which look plural but are in fact singular, and vice versa.
- to introduce students to certain nouns which refer to groups of people that can be either singular or plural.
- to practise certain nouns which are countable in many languages, but not in English.
- to introduce students to certain nouns which have a change in meaning when used as either a countable or uncountable noun.

- Write the following sentences on the board, and ask students to discuss if they are right or wrong.

  The staff is not going to accept the pay offer.
  The staff are going to buy a leaving present for Joe.
  The Brazilian team is winning at the moment.
  The team are celebrating their famous victory.

  Explain that all are possible. If you think of the group as a whole, it is singular. If you think of all the individual people who make up the group, it can be plural. The singular form is more common.

- Students work in groups to make sentences from the charts. They have some choice but not a lot.

Answers
The news is boring.
The police are coming.
The trousers are awful.
The government is trying hard at the moment.
Politics is a difficult subject.
The team is winning.
The scissors are sharp.
Mathematics is a difficult subject.
The staff is/are unhappy at the decision.
People are interesting.

- Students work in pairs to correct the sentences in question 1.

Answers
a. *some information*
b. *any good advice*
c. *an interesting news item*

d. *a lot of fruit, much of which is exported.*
e. *My luggage is*

- Students work in pairs to write two sentences for each word.

Sample answers
The chair is made of wood.
There is a big wood on top of the hill.

Nothing replaces experience in life.
The book is about my experiences in Africa.

Would you like a glass of wine?
Cinderella's shoes were made of glass.

Can I borrow your rubber? I've made a mistake.
Car tyres are made of rubber.

Would you like some cake?
I baked a cake this morning.

It's made of iron.
Careful! The iron's hot.

Time flies.
How many times have you been to America?

It is a custom in our house to have beer for breakfast.
It took hours to get through Customs. They were searching everybody.

A bar of chocolate
A box of chocolates

My arm hurts.
The soldiers had plenty of arms and ammunition.

Have you got any paper? I have to write a letter.
Could you buy a paper while you're out?

It'll only take a minute.
I will read the minutes of the last meeting.

There is a Progress Test on the whole of *Headway Upper-Intermediate* in the Workbook.

74

HEADWAY

John & Liz Soars

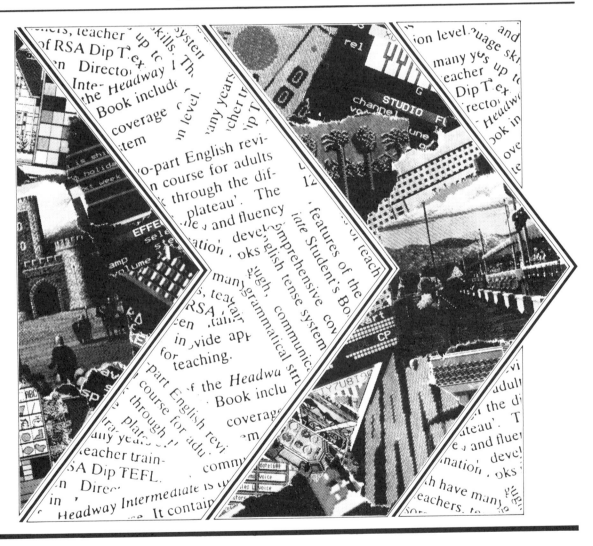

UPPER-INTERMEDIATE　　　　**TEST BOOKLET**

Note to the teacher

There are three tests in this booklet.

Progress Test One covers the work done in Units 1–4.
Progress Test Two covers the work done in Units 5–8.
Progress Test Three covers the work done in Units 9–12.

Each test carries with it a total possible score of 100 marks.

The centre pages containing the KEY can be pulled out before the test booklet is handed over to the student.

Oxford University Press
Walton Street, Oxford OX2 6DP

© Oxford University Press 1989
Typeset by VAP Publishing Services
Printed in Hong Kong

Illustrations by RDH Artists

UNITS 1-4

Progress Test One

Exercise 1 Tenses and verb forms
Put the verb in brackets in the correct tense or verb form.
You must also decide if the verb should be active or passive.

Haunted house for sale with floating tenants

There are lots of spine-chilling extras waiting for whoever buys the thirteenth-century Chingle Hall near Preston, Lancashire.

The hall, which is the oldest surviving brick-built residence in the country, (a) _____ (say) to be the most haunted house in Britain. It

(b) _____ (sell) by the international auctioneers, Sotheby's. The owners expect

(c) _____ (sell) the house for about £300,000.

A monk, a Roman soldier, a boy who hanged himself and a ghost (d) _____ all _____ (see) at various times over the centuries. Not only this, but residents

(e) _____ also _____ (hear) heavy footsteps and mysterious knockings, and

(f) _____ (feel) cold spots in warm rooms.

The hall (g) _____ (build) in 1260 by Alan de Singleton, and it (h) _____ (have) a remarkable history ever since. Oliver Cromwell is said (i) _____ (stay) at the house on the eve of the Battle of Preston in 1648, and the hall may have been the scene of the capture of at least one Royalist sympathizer, as the sound of a running horse and the rattle of a soldier's equipment

(j) _____ (hear) in the lane outside.

In the 1920s, the hall was the home of the Longton

family. Their son wanted to marry a local girl, but his father refused (k) _____ (let) him (l) _____ (do) this. Today the boy's ghost haunts the barn where he hanged himself.

Henry Soaper (m) _____ (live) in the hall for the past ten years. Some time after they moved in, while the house (n) _____ (restore), they found ancient fireplaces, timber from Viking ships and an old chapel. 'I (o) _____ (read) that there are secret hiding places somewhere,' he said. 'We (p) _____ (look) for them for years, but we (q) _____ (not find) them yet.'

He went on, 'One day, my daughter (r) _____ (go) upstairs when she said she saw a Roman soldier coming down. She stopped (s) _____ (go) up, and tried (t) _____ (turn) round, but she couldn't move. The soldier walked straight through her. We didn't really believe her until a few years later, a guest who was being shown round asked if he could photograph a 'cold' spot. The developed film showed the image of a Roman soldier reflected in a mirror.'

Total 20

Exercise 2 Question formation

Make questions from the following statements, asking about the words in italics.

Example
Who are you looking at?
*I'm looking at **that man**.*

a. _____ ?
   A very strange man lives in that house.

b. _____ ?
   I stayed at *the Paradise Hotel*.

c. _____ ?
   Dorothy's *quite tall, with short red hair. She's really nice.*

d. _____ ?
   The Independent newspaper has the best coverage of world news.

e. _____ ?
   My mother's *very well,* thank you.

f. _____
   A lot of decoration needs doing to our new house.

g. _____
   I take *size 40* shoes.

h. _____
   The film was directed by *Peter Lorenzo.*

i. _____
   I want to talk to you about *last night's meeting.*

j. _____
   I like *jazz and blues.*

Total 10

Exercise 3 Reported questions

Report the questiona a. – e. from exercise 2.

Example
She asked me who I was looking at.

a. She asked me who _____

b. She asked me _____

c. She wanted to know _____

d. He asked her _____

e. They asked me _____

Total 5

Exercise 4 Question tags

Say if the question tags in the following sentences rise or fall. Put R (rise) or F (fall) after each sentence.

a. It's a lovely day, isn't it? _____

b. You haven't seen my book anywhere, have you? _____

c. Learning English isn't always easy, is it? _____

d. Tests are horrible, aren't they? _____

e. You haven't finished *War and Peace* already, have you? I only lent it to you yesterday! _____

Total 5

Exercise 5 Correcting mistakes

The following letter is from Thomas, a Swiss student, to his old English teacher, Jenny. Unfortunately, he makes quite a few mistakes! Read the letter, and find the mistakes. Put the correct version in the column on the right. There are twenty mistakes.

© Oxford University Press `Photocopiable`

Lindenstr. 15
5430 Wettinger
Switzerland
14 February

Dear Jenny

I finally arrive home! The journey has taken thirty hours. I got here on twelve February, two days ago, and it is very nice, but a bit strange, be back home. All my family are well. I remembered buying them all a present before leave England, but I forgot to bring the presents with me! I'll try getting in touch with my old flat-mate, and ask him send them to me.

I left without say thank-you to you. You are a very good teacher. I enjoy very much. I always was interesting in your lessons. I won't stop to learn English now I'm home - I'm going to go to school here. My village doesn't have got an English school, but the town nearby is having one or two good ones.

I'd like that you do something for me, if you wouldn't mind. Could you write a reference for me and send me it at the address above? I'd be very grateful. I need it to give to the school I used to going to. They want to know how long did I stay in England, and what level was I.

I hope you're well. Write to me if you can. I look forward to hearing from you.

With best wishes,

Thomas.

Thomas

Total 20

Exercise 6   Vocabulary

Fill the gaps and answer the questions with words that appeared in the first four units of Headway Upper-Intermediate. Each dash (___) represents one letter. The first letter of each word is provided as a clue.

a. Esperanto isn't a real language, it's an

a _ _ _ _ _ _ _ _ _ _ one.

b. What's the name of the reference book, usually quite big, that gives information about people, places and

things? e _ _ _ _ _ _ _ _ _ _

c. What is the line of hair above your eyes

called? e _ _ _ _ _ _ .

d. What's the name of the place where ships are loaded

and unloaded? d _ _ _ _ .

e. What's the word for a financial plan where a company or a government decides how much money

to spend on different things? b _ _ _ _ _ _ .

f. If you have a minus amount of money in the bank,

your account is o _ _ _ _ _ _ _ _ .

g. This is where actors stand in the

theatre. s _ _ _ _ .

h. A verb meaning to walk quietly and slowly. This is how the boy went to school in Shakespeare's *Seven ages of man*! c _ _ _ _ _ .

i. The opinion that other people have of you is your

r _ _ _ _ _ _ _ _ _ .

j. If a photo makes someone look more attractive than in fact they are, we say it is a

f _ _ _ _ _ _ _ _ _ picture.

k. If you are absolutely certain of something, you are

c _ _ _ _ _ _ _ of it.

l. If you are pleased because someone has done

something for you, you are g _ _ _ _ _ _ _
to them.

m. A hammer, a screwdriver and a saw are all examples

of t _ _ _ _ .

n. What's the word for the amount of money you get from your employer as well as your usual salary, as a

reward or gift? b _ _ _ _ .

o. This kind of work needs quite a lot of training and ability. s _ _ _ _ _ _ .

p. A job which needs effort and determination is this, and you feel good if you do well in

it. c _ _ _ _ _ _ _ _ _ .

q. The things that you manage to do in life or in your job

are called your a _ _ _ _ _ _ _ _ _ _ _ .

r. If you take a lot of care to avoid danger, you are a

c _ _ _ _ _ _ _ person.

s. Another word for *tremble*. People do this if they are

cold or frightened. s _ _ _ _ _ .

t. If I give you my book and you give me your book, we

have s _ _ _ _ _ _ _ books.

Total 20

Exercise 7   Nouns and verbs

The following nouns can all be used as verbs. Write a sentence which contains the word used as a verb.

a. water _____

b. head _____

c. time _____

d. finger _____

e. back _____

Total 5

Exercise 8   Compound nouns

Answer the questions with a compound noun formed with either **eye**, **finger** or **head**.

a. Someone who actually sees a crime is called

this. _____

b. The main building of an organization is called

its _____ .

c. These are what you put over your ears if you want to listen to music without disturbing other

people. _____

d. If the police suspect you of a crime, they might take

your _____ s and see if they match with those found at the scene of the crime.

e. If you are making progress with something, we can

say that you are making _____

Total 5

Exercise 9   Opposites

Form the opposite of the following adjectives, using one of the prefixes.

in- il- dis- un-

a. willing

© Oxford University Press Photocopiable

b. legal   —————————————

c. correct   —————————————

d. efficient   —————————————

e. honest   —————————————

Total 5

Exercise 10   Pronunciation

In the following lists of words, three words rhyme.
Underline the one that is different.

Example
ghost <u>lost</u> most post

a. break steak weak great
b. sew through few shoe
c. choose lose news loose
d. cord word heard third
e. comb home Rome bomb

Total 5

Score

Exercise 1 —— out of 20
Exercise 2 —— out of 10
Exercise 3 —— out of 5
Exercise 4 —— out of 5
Exercise 5 —— out of 20
Exercise 6 —— out of 20
Exercise 7 —— out of 5
Exercise 8 —— out of 5
Exercise 9 —— out of 5
Exercise 10 —— out of 5

Total   ——
       100

Percentage
Total   [/ %]

UNITS 5-8

Progress Test Two

Exercise 1   Tenses and verb forms

Put the verb in brackets in the correct tense or verb form.
You must also decide if the verb should be active or passive.

Holiday Misery at Gatwick Airport

Another night of chaos for passengers stranded at Gatwick airport.

The strike by Greek air traffic controllers

(a) _____ (call off) late last night, but

thousands of holidaymakers   (b) _____

still _____ (suffer) at airports throughout

Britain. 3,000 tourists   (c) _____
(spend) their third night last night

(d) _____ (camp) out at Gatwick
Airport. One of the airport's main restaurants

(e) _____ (close) and 50 families with

children   (f) _____ (sleep) there. A

lucky few   (g) _____ (anticipate) delays

and   (h) _____ (bring) games and
cushions to ease the pain and boredom for the children.
However by early today the restaurant area

(i) _____ (look) like a refugee camp,

with passengers   (j) _____ (lie) among
piles of baggage and rubbish.

The airport operation manager, Christine Morrow, said

that the situation   (k) _____
(deteriorate) dramatically in the last 24 hours, despite

the fact that the strike   (l) _____

6

(end). She expects that it   (m) _____
(take) at least 4 days   (n) _____
(clear) the backlog of flights and that the general

situation   (o) _____ (return) to normal
by the middle of next week. However while she

(p) _____ (make) a statement to the
press there   (q) _____ (come) news
that French and Spanish air traffic controllers

(r) _____ (meet) tomorrow to consider
possible strike action. They say that their job

(s) _____ (become) impossible in recent
years because of the increase in the number of flights

(t) _____ (demand) by greedy tour
operators at peak holiday times.

It seems both travellers and air traffic controllers deserve
our sympathy!

Total 20

Exercise 2   Narrative tenses

In the following sentences sometimes *only one* and
sometimes *both* of the tenses in brackets are correct.
Underline the correct one(s).

a. Jane (**lived/had lived**) with her aunt since the age of
    three.
b. They (**studied/were studying**) their notes when the
    teacher came in.
c. She ran out into the sunshine as soon as she
    (**finished/had finished**) her work.
d. (**Did you study/Were you studying**) French at
    Durham University?
e. He didn't stop running until he (**reached/had
    reached**) home.
f. She (**had read/had been reading**) all morning
    without understanding one word.
g. They (**were having/had had**) breakfast when I
    came downstairs.
h. How many pints of beer (**had he drunk/had he been
    drinking**) when he passed out?
i. Although she (**attended/had attended**) church
    regularly as a child, she rarely went as an adult.
j. I (**didn't see/hadn't seen**) him before he left for
    Athens.

Total 10

Exercise 3   Future Forms

Complete the following dialogue using the verb in
brackets in a suitable future form.

A: What time   (a) _____ the plane
    _____ (leave) tomorrow?
B: Not until 7 o'clock in the evening, but of
    course we have to be there an hour before

    that, so I   (b) _____ (order) a taxi to
    pick us up at 4 o'clock. I can't wait! Tomorrow night

    we   (c) _____ (sleep) in the Plaza Hotel
    with the moonlight shining across the sea and into
    our bedroom window.

A: I   (d) _____ (not pack) until tomorrow

    morning then.   (e) _____ your mother
    _____ (come) round to say goodbye?

B: No, she can't. She   (f) _____ (help)
    Aunt May and Uncle Bill. They

    (g) _____ (move) house the day after
    tomorrow, if you remember. They

    (h) _____ completely _____
    (settle) into their new house by the time we get back
    from holiday.

A: Sh! SHSHSH! Look at the news on the T.V.! Oh,
    no! The air traffic controllers have gone on strike!

    We   (i) _____ (not go) anywhere at 7
    o'clock tomorrow! There's no chance of a flight
    anywhere until next weekend! Oh dear – I think I

    (j) _____ (cry)!

Total 10

Exercise 4   Mass and count nouns

Rewrite the following sentences using the word in
brackets. Make any necessary changes.

a. There have been few advances in the health care of
    children in developing countries. (progress)

    _____

b. He didn't give me many details about the job.
    (information)

    _____

c. How many hours have been spent doing this? (time)

    _____

d. A great deal of research has been done.
    (experiments)

    _____

e. He has fewer ideas than she does. (knowledge)

Total 5

Exercise 5   Correcting Mistakes

In each of the following sentences there are two **grammatical** mistakes.

Find them and correct them.

a. He was a very brilliant tennis player until he'd had that bad fall when he was playing in the final at Wimbledon.

b. She's had a great deal of jobs over the last few years; I hope she'll be finding a permanent one soon.

c. He believes that every Western medicine is ineffective and that everybody has to go to an acupuncturist regularly.

d. You mustn't pick me up from the station if you don't want to. I always think getting a taxi is excited.

e. The writer Somerset Maugham that died in the sixties, often wrote about the boredom of a routine existence despite his own life was very exciting.

f. The life-guard could save the drowned child because of his excellent training in first aid.

g. I'm really sorry I can't get to your dinner party but I'll leave for Stockholm the next day, and I've got several packing to do.

h. I recognised him very easily because he had absolutely big ears, and wearing a turquoise tie.

i. I couldn't find somebody whose knowledge of the subject impressing me very much.

j. I hadn't received the information I sent away for although enclosing a stamped addressed envelope.

Total 20

Exercise 6   Vocabulary – a crossword

All the words in the crossword appeared in Units 5–8 of Headway Upper-Intermediate. Solve the clues and complete the crossword. Some of the clues refer to homonyms and homophones. Remember that homonyms are words with the same spelling but different meanings (a **bank** for money and the **bank** of a river), and homophones are words with the same pronunciation but different meanings (**plane** and **plain**).

ACROSS

1. This flies without an engine. (6)
4. An old, dirty and dilapidated place to live. (4)
5. The doctor (for example) gives you this with a *c*, but this is the verb with an *s*. (6)
8. Prince Charles is a homophone for *air*, because one day he'll be King. (4)
9. A verb which means to *breathe in*. (6)
10. A _____ of jam. (3)
13. An army vehicle. (4)
15. A line of old age on the face. (7)
16. A shape which isn't quite round. (4)
17. A _____ of toothpaste. (4)

DOWN

1. A sticky substance. (4)
2. You throw this in some board games, and *to _____ with death* means to act dangerously. (4)
3. *Raw* vegetables – the homophone is the noise lions make. (4)
4. A homonym – it's a kind of bird, or it's what you do when you eat. (7)
6. This is bigger than a car but smaller than a lorry. (3)
7. This means to *look long and hard* and its homophone is something you climb. (5)
11. If it's another word for *rubbish*, the stress pattern is Oo; if it's the opposite of to *accept*, the stress pattern is oO. (6)
12. This is a homophone of *higher*, and it's what you do if you want a car for a few days or weeks. (4)
14. A cat has a *paw*, and the homophone means the tiny hole that you have all over your skin. (4)

Total 20

Exercise 7   Vocabulary and common expressions

Complete the following dialogue in a doctor's surgery. Where the first letter of the missing word is given, fill the gap with one suitable word.

Example

*a walk in the **p**ark*

Where there is just a gap, choose a suitable expression from the list below the dialogue. Careful! Not all the expressions are used!

Doctor: Take a seat. What seems to be the trouble? Can you describe your   (a) **s** _____ ?

Patient: Well, I thought at first it was food (b) **p** _____ because I was very sick in the middle of the night. I felt really (c) **d** _____ and I thought I was going to faint. Then this morning I woke with this (d) **r** _____ all over my body. It can't be measles. I'm sure I had measles when I was a child.

© Oxford University Press Photocopiable

Doctor: (e) _____ . Most people get measles when they are young. Let me examine you. Is it painful when you swallow, because your glands seem to be a bit (f) **s** _____ ?

Patient: Yes, a little bit. (g) _____ ! That hurts!

Doctor: (h) _____ ! Well, I'm pretty sure what the trouble is – you're allergic to something. Did you eat anything yesterday that you don't normally eat?

Patient: No, (i) _____ . Wait a minute! I had strawberries for the first time this year, but I've never reacted to them before.

Doctor: It can happen like that. Funnily enough, there seems to have been a (j) **s** _____ increase in the numbers of those suffering from allergies this year. No one knows why. Here's a prescription, anyway. It should clear up very soon.

Patient: Thanks very much, Doctor.

Expressions

Pardon?	**Sorry!**
I hope not.	**Watch out!**
I don't think so.	**I expect you did.**
Ouch!	**Ugh!**
What, again?	**It serves you right.**

Total 10

Exercise 8   Pronunciation – word stress

In the following sentences mark the stress in the words in italics.

Example
You're making good 'progress

a. The *convicts protested* about the terrible conditions in the prison.
b. He was *convicted* for being a drug *addict*.
c. He'd been *addicted* ever since he *deserted* from the army.
d. His thirst *increased* with every step he took across burning *desert*.
e. There's been a sharp *increase* in the numbers of people who are interested in *ecology*.

Total 5

Score

Exercise 1	_____	out of 20
Exercise 2	_____	out of 10
Exercise 3	_____	out of 10
Exercise 4	_____	out of 5
Exercise 5	_____	out of 20
Exercise 6	_____	out of 20
Exercise 7	_____	out of 10
Exercise 8	_____	out of 5

Total _____

100

Percentage Total ⬚ %

9

Progress Test Three

Exercise 1   Tenses, verb forms and gap fill

In the following article there a number of gaps. After some gaps there is a verb in brackets.
Put the verb in the correct tense or verb form.

Example

Yesterday I _____*went*_____ (go) to the park.

When there is no verb in brackets, put in **one** suitable
word – perhaps a modal verb (**will**, **would**, **might**), an
article, etc.

Example

The sun rises in _____*the*_____ east.

In the article, which is from a magazine, a well-known
person describes his/her childhood relationship with a
close relative.

Phil Collins, rock star and actor, and his brother Clive, cartoonist, talk to Linda Newman.

Phil Collins, 37, is one of the world's biggest rock stars. It
is estimated that with Genesis he   **(a)** _____
(sell) over 50 million records over the past 16 years. He
also stars in a film, *Buster*, which   **(b)** _____
(release) next September. Clive Collins, 46, is a cartoonist
(c) _____ work regularly appears in
newspapers and magazines.

Phil Collins: Clive and I   **(d)** _____ to share
a bedroom with bunk beds. There was a light switch by
the bed, and when Clive came to bed, he was supposed
to switch it off. I remember   **(e)** _____
(wake) up one night and seeing the switch on fire. It was
lucky that I did. If one of us   **(f)** _____ (not
wake) up, we   **(g)** _____ have been killed.

© Oxford University Press Photocopiable

We all had our own interests. As far back as I can remember, Clive was always drawing – he (h) _____ spend whole weekends doing sketches, which were then stuck all over the bedroom walls. As soon as I came home from school, I started practising on my drums. I have always told the story that when I was 12, I sold my train set and put the money towards a drum kit. But I (i) _____ just _____ (find) out that it was Clive's set, so it wasn't my sacrifice at all! I'd say that if he had a weakness, it's that he's too modest. He wins a lot of awards, but he (j) _____ (not tell) anyone.

He (k) _____ hide them away and not say anything. It's so typical of him!

Clive Collins: I (l) _____ always _____ (think) of Phil as my kid brother. At home, he was always playing the drums. He (m) _____ (have) a set when he was 3 or 4, and Mother (n) _____ to pay £3 (o) _____ hour for him to have lessons. As soon as he started practising, the neighbours (p) _____ ring the police to complain about (q) _____ noise, but I got (r) _____ to it and didn't notice. We don't see as much of each other as we'd like. He (s) _____ always _____ (fly) off around the world giving concerts, because he works very hard. I wish we (t) _____ (live) a little closer to each other.

Total 20

Exercise 2 Tenses and verb forms

Finish each of the following sentences in such a way that it means exactly the same as the original sentence.

Example

I'm sure she's French.

*She must **be French**.*

a. I am sorry that I was so rude to her.

I wish _____ .

b. I didn't apologize. This was wrong of me.

I should _____ .

c. I'm sure it was Judy that I saw in town this morning.

It must _____ .

d. I couldn't speak to her, so I didn't ask her how she was.

If I _____ .

e. Why is the postman ringing the doorbell? Perhaps he's delivering the books I ordered.

Why is the postman ringing the doorbell? He

might _____

_____ .

f. No, I'm sure it's not the books. I only ordered them yesterday.

It can't _____ .

g. I hope they come soon.

I wish _____ .

h. I have so little time to read.

I wish _____ .

i. I have to work at weekends, so I can't read then, either.

If I _____ .

j. James hasn't rung me. Perhaps he tried to get me while I was out.

James hasn't rung me. He could _____

· _____ .

Total 10

Exercise 3 Verb patterns in reported speech

Report the following direct speech, using the verb suggested.

a. 'I'm sorry I'm late.'

She apologized _____ .

b. 'I'll pay you back as soon as I can,' he said to his father.

He promised _____

c. 'Let me tell you how to get to my house,' she said to Anne.

She explained _____ .

d. 'I can't work at all! My typewriter isn't working properly,' she said.

She complained _____

e. 'The plane will be taking off in a few minutes.'

It was announced _____ .

f. 'No, no! Please let me pay for the meal!' Pat said.

Pat insisted _____

g. 'I'll lend you the money you need,' Liz said to her daughter.

Liz agreed _____.

h. 'I most certainly will not resign!' said the director.

The director refused _____.

i. 'I'll give you a lift, if you like,' he said to Jane.

He offered _____.

j. 'I think you should try to be more punctual,' she said to Peter.

She suggested _____.

Total 10

Exercise 4   Articles

Fill the gaps in the following sentences with **a**, **the** or nothing.

a. As I was taking my children to _____ school this

morning, I noticed that there was _____ long

queue outside _____ post office.

b. I heard on _____ radio that there was _____

traffic jam on _____ road I normally take to

_____ work, so I took another route, and I

managed to avoid _____ traffic jam completely.

c. I got to _____ office in _____ good time, and

said hello to _____ doorman. My colleague and I

were going over _____ day's agenda when there

was _____ phone call for me. 'There's _____
Mr Smith from Bradfield who's come to see you.

He's waiting in _____ Reception.'

Total 15

Exercise 5   Correcting mistakes

In the following sentences there are mistakes of grammar and vocabulary. Find them and correct them.

a. **Customer in a restaurant**: I have controlled the bill, and I think you must do a mistake. I didn't have a champagne.

b. The Republicans are usually the more popular party in America, but actually the Democratic Party is winning. Their share of the vote has raised to fifty-six per cent.

c. I have been expecting you for ages! What have you been doing? I thought you couldn't remember that

we had a meeting. I was going to ring you yesterday to remember you, but I was sure you wouldn't forget.

d. The dress suited her perfectly, but the style didn't fit her at all. If I hadn't have told her, she would have been buying it.

e. Peter doesn't do as much sport as he used to it. Last week we went mountain climbing, and he soon got tired. I didn't, because I'm used to.

Total 15

Exercise 6   Vocabulary

Fill the gaps and answer the questions with words that appeared in units 9–12 of Headway Upper-Intermediate. Each dash (_) represents one letter. The first letter of each word is provided as a clue.

a. If you close a door very forcefully, you s _____ it.

b. A person who always remembers your birthday is

very t _____.

c. If you can't stop thinking about something, you are

o _____ with it.

d. Another word for a prize, for example, one given to

writers. a _____

e. A person who is always ready to attack other people is this. The opposite is peaceful.

a _____

f. A person who refuses to change his/her mind is this. Mules and donkeys are said to be this!

o _____

g. A person who eats more than their fair share is

this! g _____

h. A person who doesn't tell the truth is this.

d _____

i. The money that you pay to release someone who has

been kidnapped is called the r _____.

j. There are two main types of bank account, a

c _____ account and a

d _____ account.

k. Another word for the top of a mountain. p _____

l. The time or date before which a particular job must

be done is called the d _____.

m. Another word for delay, for example, on the

underground or on a motorway. h _____

n. The day after you've done a lot of exercise, your

arms and legs might feel s _____.

Total 15

Exercise 7   Multi-word verbs

Choose a word in column A and an adverb/preposition in column B to complete the gaps. Put the verb in the correct form.

A	B
find	after
go (× 2)	across
tell	off
take	down
get	up
break	out
eat	
come	
show	

a. 'What terminal does the flight leave from?'

'I don't know. I'll _____ _____ for you.'

b. They didn't put enough coal on the fire, and it

_____ _____ while they were asleep.

c. Also, they didn't put the meat in the fridge, and by the time they came to cook it, it had

_____ _____ , so they had to throw it away.

d. My daughter has gone into acting and the theatre just as I did, so I suppose she has

_____ _____ me more than her father.

e. I _____ _____ my first love letter while I was looking for my passport. What a lovely letter it was!

f. The little girl was _____ _____ by her parents because she had ruined her new clothes.

g. Come on! _____ _____ your lunch before it gets cold!

h. Nick's a nice boy, but I wish he wouldn't

_____ _____ about how incredibly wealthy his parents are. We all know they're millionaires, so he doesn't have to go on about it.

i. Brian's relationship with Stephanie

_____ _____ because they simply didn't trust each other.

j. I feel terribly _____ _____ by my children. None of them has done anything worthwhile with their lives.

Total 10

Exercise 8   Sentence stress

In the following dialogues, underline where the main stress is in B's replies.

Example
A: *I thought you didn't like cake.*
B: *I adore cake.*

a. **A:** Who did you tell about the party?
   B: I told Peter.
b. **A:** I lost all my money playing cards.
   B: I told you.
c. **A:** Who told Alice that I'd been sacked?
   B: I told her.
d. **A:** Have you paid the gas bill yet?
   B: I thought you'd paid it!
e. **A:** Don't worry about the gas bill. I've paid it.
   B: I thought you had.

Total 5

Score

Exercise 1 _____	out of 20
Exercise 2 _____	out of 10
Exercise 3 _____	out of 10
Exercise 4 _____	out of 15
Exercise 5 _____	out of 15
Exercise 6 _____	out of 15
Exercise 7 _____	out of 10
Exercise 8 _____	out of 5

Total _____

100

Percentage Total [____ / ____ %]

KEY

Test 1   Units 1–4

Exercise 1

a. is said
b. is being sold
c. to sell
d. have all been seen
e. have also heard
f. have felt
g. was built
h. has had
i. to have stayed
j. have been heard
k. to let
l. do
m. has lived/has been living
n. was being restored
o. have read
p. have been looking/have looked
q. haven't found
r. was going
s. going
t. to turn

Exercise 2

a. Who lives in that house?
b. Which hotel did you stay at?
c. What's Dorothy like?
d. Which newspaper has the best coverage of world news?
e. How's your mother?
f. What needs doing to your new house?
g. What size shoes do you take?
h. Who was the film directed by?/Who directed the film?
i. What do you want to talk to me about?
j. What sort of music do you like?

Exercise 3

a. She asked me who lived in that house.
b. She asked me which hotel I stayed/had stayed at.
c. She wanted to know what Dorothy was like.
d. He asked her which newspaper had the best coverage of world news.
e. They asked me how my mother was.

Exercise 4

a. F   d. F
b. R   e. R
c. F

Exercise 5

I have finally arrived
The journey took
on the twelfth of February/on February 12
to be back home
I remembered to buy
before leaving
I'll try to get
ask him to send
without saying
I enjoyed your lessons/I enjoyed being in your class
I was always
interested
I won't stop learning
village hasn't got/doesn't have
town nearby has/has got
I'd like you to do
send it to me
the school I used to go to
how long I stayed
what level I was

Exercise 6

a. artificial
b. encyclopaedia
c. eyebrow
d. dock
e. budget
f. overdrawn
g. stage
h. creep
i. reputation
j. flattering
k. convinced
l. grateful
m. tools
n. bonus
o. skilled
p. challenging
q. achievements
r. cautious
s. shiver
t. swapped

Exercise 7

Sample answers

a. You have to water flowers.
b. The footballer headed the ball into the net.
c. When you are cooking, you have to time things carefully.
d. She fingered the material lovingly.
e. I backed the car out of the garage.

Exercise 8

a. eyewitness
b. headquarters
c. headphones
d. fingerprints
e. headway

Exercise 9

a. unwilling
b. illegal
c. incorrect
d. inefficient
e. dishonest

Exercise 10

a. weak
b. sew
c. loose
d. cord
e. bomb

Test 2   Units 5–8

Exercise 1

a. was called off
b. are still suffering
c. spent
d. camping/camped
e. was closed
f. slept
g. had anticipated
h. had brought
i. looked/was looking
j. lying
k. had deteriorated
l. had ended
m. will take
n. to clear
o. will have returned
p. was making
q. came
r. are meeting/are going to meet/will meet
s. has become
t. demanded

Exercise 2

a. had lived
b. both (but there is a change in meaning)
c. both
d. Did you study? (**Were you studying?** is possible but less likely.)
e. both
f. had been reading
g. both (but there is a change in meaning)
h. had he drunk
i. attended
j. didn't see

Exercise 3

a. does the plane leave
b. will order
c. will be sleeping
d. won't pack
e. Is your mother coming round?/Is your mother going to come round/Will your mother be coming round?
f. is helping/is going to help/will be helping
g. are moving
h. will have completely settled
i. won't be going
j. am going to cry

Exercise 4

a. There has been little progress in the health care of children in developing countries.
b. He didn't give me much information about the job.
c. How much time has been spent doing this?
d. A large number of/A great many experiments have been done.
e. He has less knowledge than she does.

Exercise 5

a. an absolutely/really brilliant tennis player
   he had that bad fall
b. a great many/a large number of
   she'll find
c. all Western medicine
   everybody should go
d. You don't have to/You don't need to
   is exciting
e. The writer Somerset Maugham, who died in the sixties,
   although his own life was very exciting
f. was able to save/managed to save
   drowning
g. I'm leaving/I leave
   some packing
h. very big ears
   he was wearing
i. anybody
   impressed
j. I didn't receive/haven't received
   despite/although I enclosed

Exercise 6

Exercise 7

a. symptoms   e. I expect you did.   i. I don't think so.
b. poisoning   f. swollen   j. sharp
c. dizzy   g. Ouch!
d. rash   h. Sorry!

Exercise 8

a. 'convicts   c. ad'dicted   e. 'increase
    pro'tested   de'serted   e'cology
b. con'victed   d. in'creased
    'addict   'desert

Test 3   Units 9–12

Exercise 1

a. has sold
b. will be released/is being released
c. whose
d. used
e. waking
f. hadn't woken
g. might/could/may/would
h. would
i. have just found
j. doesn't tell/won't tell
k. 'll (The uncontracted form **will** is possible, but the contraction is best.)
l. have always thought
m. had
n. used
o. an
p. would
q. the
r. used
s. is always flying
t. lived

Exercise 2

a. I wish I hadn't been so rude to her.
b. I should have apologized.
c. It must have been Judy I saw in town this morning.
d. If I had been able to speak to her, I would have asked her how she was.
e. He might be delivering the books I ordered.
f. It can't be the books.
g. I wish they would come soon.
h. I wish I had more time to read.
i. If I didn't have to work at weekends, I could read then.
j. He could have tried to ring me while I was out.

Exercise 3

a. She apologized for being late.
b. He promised to pay back his father as soon as he could.
c. She explained to Anne how to get to her house.
d. She complained that she couldn't work because her typewriter wasn't working properly.
e. It was announced that the plane would be taking off in a few minutes.
f. Pat insisted that he/she paid for the meal./Pat insisted on paying for the meal.
g. Liz agreed to lend her daughter the money she needed.
h. The director refused to resign.
i. He offered to give Jane a lift.
j. She suggested that Peter should try to be more punctual.

Exercise 4

a. (nothing) a the
b. the a the (nothing) the
c. the (nothing) the the a a (nothing)

Exercise 5

a. checked the bill   you must have made a mistake   have champagne
b. at the moment the Democratic Party is winning   has risen
c. have been waiting for you   I thought you may/might not have remembered/may/might have forgotten   to remind you
d. dress fitted her   style didn't suit   I hadn't told her   would have brought
e. as he used to   I'm used to it

Exercise 6

a. slam   h. deceitful
b. thoughtful   i. ransom
c. obsessed   j. current deposit
d. award   k. peak
e. aggressive   l. deadline
f. obstinate   m. hold-up
g. greedy   n. stiff

Exercise 7

a. find out   f. told off
b. went out   g. Eat up
c. gone off   h. show off
d. taken after   i. broke up
e. came across   j. let down

Exercise 8

Stressed words

a. Peter   d. you'd
b. told   e. thought
c. I